WHAT'S THE POINT OF
PHILOSOPHY?

Penguin Random House

Designer Anna Pond
Senior Editors Sam Atkinson, Pauline Savage
Project Editor Kelsie Besaw
Project Art Editor Joe Lawrence
Editor Zaina Budaly
US Editors Lori Hand, Jenny Wilson
Illustrator Sanya Jain
Consultant Marcus Weeks
Writers Sam Atkinson, Kelsie Besaw, Pauline Savage

Managing Editor Rachel Fox
Managing Art Editor Owen Peyton Jones
Production Controller Laura Andrews
Production Editor Jacqueline Street-Elkayam
UK Media Archive Romaine Werblow
Jacket Designers Akiko Kato, Juhi Sheth
DTP Designer Rakesh Kumar
Senior Jackets Coordinator Priyanka Sharma-Saddi
Jacket Design Development Manager Sophia MTT

Publisher Andrew Macintyre
Art Director Karen Self
Associate Publishing Director Liz Wheeler
Publishing Director Jonathan Metcalf

First American Edition, 2022
Published in the United States by DK Publishing
1745 Broadway, New York, NY 10019

Copyright © 2022 Dorling Kindersley Limited
DK, a Division of Penguin Random House LLC
22 23 24 25 26 10 9 8 7 6 5 4 3 2 1
001-326785-Aug/2022

A catalog record for this book
is available from the Library of Congress.
ISBN 978-0-7440-5624-2

DK books are available at special discounts when purchased
in bulk for sales promotions, premiums, fund-raising, or educational
use. For details, contact: DK Publishing Special Markets,
1745 Broadway, Suite 801, New York, NY 10019
SpecialSales@dk.com

Printed and bound in China

For the curious
www.dk.com

This book was made with Forest Stewardship
Council™ certified paper – one small step
in DK's commitment to a sustainable future.
For more information go to
www.dk.com/our-green-pledge

WHAT'S THE POINT OF
PHILOSOPHY?

DK

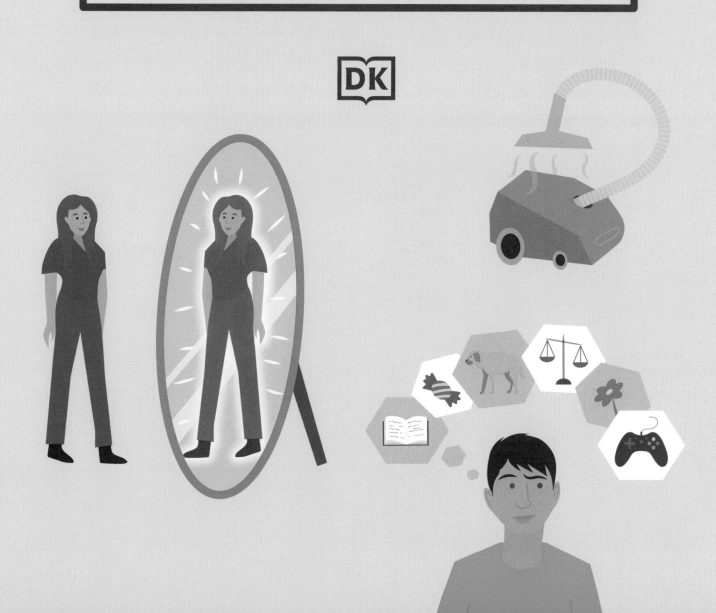

CONTENTS

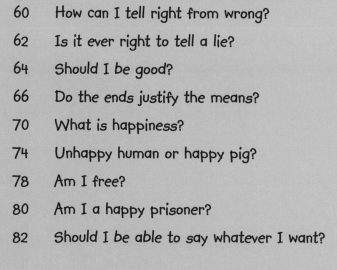
Some dates have BCE and CE after them. These are short for "before the Common Era" and "Common Era." The Common Era dates from when people think Jesus was born.

WHAT'S THE POINT OF PHILOSOPHY?

Philosophy is all about the joy of asking questions—about the world, about life, and about what kind of person you want to be—and not always getting an answer! People of all ages love philosophy for its own sake, but it can also be a really useful tool to help you think clearly, use your imagination, and communicate your ideas to others.

PROBLEM-SOLVING

Philosophy was developed in the first place to try to solve life's big problems. Early philosophers broke down each problem to find its core and then explored a variety of solutions. You can apply the same technique to your own problems.

EXAMINING THE WORLD

Some questions about the world around us can't be answered by science. Is the world around us real? Why are we here? Though philosophy doesn't offer any definite answers to these questions, it's in the discussion of these ideas that philosophy teaches us about the world and our place in it.

CLEAR THINKING

Philosophical arguments are based on clear, logical reasoning. Studying philosophy and discussing it with others is good exercise for the mind. It can help you to organize your ideas on a subject and think about it more clearly.

GENERATING IDEAS

The study of ideas can help you get better at coming up with ideas of your own. By developing their thinking skills, philosophers are better able to put together new ideas when they are confronted with new situations. They are also able to think more creatively in the face of difficult challenges.

DECIDING WHAT'S RIGHT

There are whole areas of philosophy that are devoted to exploring questions about what is right and how we should treat others. Philosophers also discuss how we should treat animals, and even the planet we live on.

CHALLENGING ASSUMPTIONS

Many people go through life without questioning their beliefs. They often make assumptions—they accept something as true without really having any proof. If you study philosophy, you can learn to recognize and challenge these assumptions, whether they are held by others or by yourself.

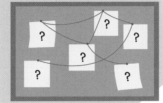

THINKING FOR YOURSELF

Being able to think independently is an important skill. The history of philosophy is full of people whose ideas went against what everyone else thought at the time, or who just started thinking about something in a totally different way.

INVESTIGATING YOUR OWN OPINIONS

Studying the opinions of other people can help you to critically examine your own opinions. By examining different philosophers' ideas on a topic, you can investigate why you think a certain way about it yourself. It's possible you might even end up changing your mind.

SEEING BOTH SIDES

Though individual philosophers may disagree with a certain viewpoint, philosophy as a whole is more concerned with presenting a wide variety of opinions. By looking at multiple points of view, you can compare their differences and even learn to recognize hidden similarities between them.

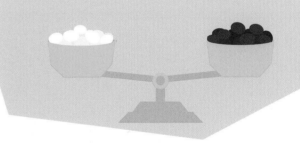

PRESENTING AN ARGUMENT

Learning about philosophy can help you to present your arguments to others in a more persuasive way. You'll also find it easier to recognize when other people are making bad arguments.

EVALUATING INFORMATION

Philosophy teaches us not to simply accept the ideas and information that are presented to us. Instead we must examine them to make sure they contain strong arguments. They should also not be biased—unfairly leaning toward a particular point of view.

TESTING YOUR IDEAS

It's not just scientists who conduct experiments. Philosophers do it, too. They come up with imaginary situations that would put their ideas to the test and then think about the possible consequences of those situations. These tests are called "thought experiments," and you can find lots of examples throughout this book.

WHAT'S THE POINT OF THINKING ABOUT
EXISTENCE?

Some of the first questions to be asked by ancient philosophers were about existence: what the universe consists of and what is our place in it. Their thoughts formed the basis of the modern sciences of physics, chemistry, and biology and led to discoveries such as the existence of atoms. Thinking about the nature of our own existence can help us to find purpose in our lives and to understand and accept the beliefs of others more easily.

WHAT'S THE SMALLEST SOMETHING CAN BE?

Some things are so small, they can only be seen under a microscope. But even these are not the smallest things that exist. Science has found things that are smaller still, particles that need special equipment to record their existence. But are some particles too small to be divided into smaller parts? Or is it possible to keep cutting things in half and not reach a point at which they become uncuttable?

1 If you keep cutting a grain of sand in half, what's the smallest piece you can divide it into? This was one of the earliest questions to be debated in philosophy, and two ancient Greek thinkers had opposing views on the idea.

Democritus thought that atoms were hard and indestructible.

2 Democritus thought that, eventually, the grain of sand would not be able to be divided any further. We would be left with small particles that he called "atoms," which put together make up everything in the universe.

REAL WORLD

Atoms
Scientists today know that everything is made up of atoms, though these atoms are different from how Democritus thought of them. They can also be split into even smaller particles.

- If something kept getting smaller, would it eventually shrink to nothing?

- Do you think that everything in the universe is made of one thing, or of many things? Why?

Aristotle thought that you could go on cutting things up forever.

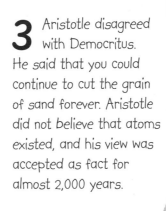

3 Aristotle disagreed with Democritus. He said that you could continue to cut the grain of sand forever. Aristotle did not believe that atoms existed, and his view was accepted as fact for almost 2,000 years.

BUILDING BLOCKS OF THE UNIVERSE

Many early philosophers in ancient Greece were interested in discovering if there is a substance that everything in the universe is made of. They called this substance the fundamental principle. The Greeks had many different ideas about what it might be, from water to fire.

For ancient Greek thinker Thales, water was the fundamental principle.

The four elements

The ancient Greek philosopher Empedocles believed that the universe was made from a mixture of four elements: fire, earth, air, and water. They could be bound together by a force he called love or broken apart by a force he called strife.

Air

Fire

Water

Earth

DOES NOTHING EXIST?

What do we mean by *something* and *nothing*? We might define "something" as anything that exists. Thinking of something might bring thoughts of anything from our family and friends to our favorite toys, books, and video games. But what comes to mind when we try to think of nothing? Do you imagine empty space, or darkness? What exactly is the definition of "nothing"? Many philosophers have wondered if it's possible for nothing to exist at all.

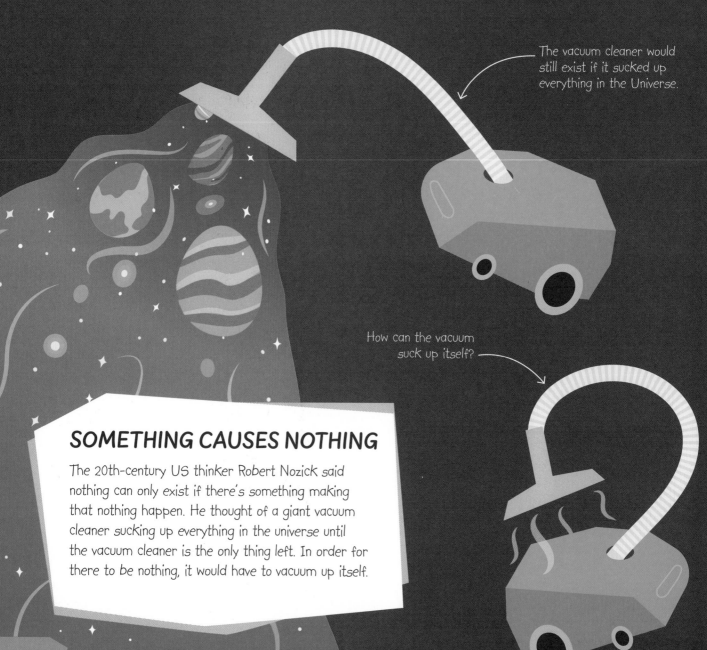

The vacuum cleaner would still exist if it sucked up everything in the Universe.

How can the vacuum suck up itself?

SOMETHING CAUSES NOTHING

The 20th-century US thinker Robert Nozick said nothing can only exist if there's something making that nothing happen. He thought of a giant vacuum cleaner sucking up everything in the universe until the vacuum cleaner is the only thing left. In order for there to be nothing, it would have to vacuum up itself.

NOTHING IS SOMETHING

In the early 1900s, French philosopher Henri Bergson said there was no such thing as nothing *because even within an empty space, we can still sense something.* If an astronaut was floating in space, they would *see blackness—that blackness is still something, so the existence of nothingness is impossible.*

DON'T THINK OF AN ELEPHANT!

The ancient Greek thinker Parmenides also argued that nothing can't exist. He said it's impossible to think of nothing because thinking about it turns it into something. If someone said to you "Don't think of an elephant!" you would find it impossible not to think of an elephant.

ZERO

The number zero is a symbol for nothingness. But ancient philosophers struggled with the concept of nothing. For centuries, this prevented the development of the number and slowed mathematical progress. When philosophers and mathematicians accepted the idea of nothingness in India in the 7th century CE, it was possible for zero to emerge.

DO UNICORNS EXIST?

Parmenides said "nothing comes from nothing," which means that something can't be created from nothing. There can only ever be "what is," never "what is not." Something that exists can't also not exist, and "something that is not" can't suddenly become "something that is." So everything must exist, and it must have existed forever. Even if unicorns aren't real creatures, they still exist as ideas in our minds.

WHAT IS REAL?

The question of what is real may seem like an odd one. After all, when we look around us, everything seems real enough, doesn't it? But the debate about the nature of the world has divided philosophy into those who think it's made of physical matter—materialists—and those who think it's all in the mind—idealists.

A MECHANICAL UNIVERSE

The 17th-century English philosopher Thomas Hobbes was a materialist. He believed that everything in the universe could be explained by the way physical objects move and interact with each other, whether they are planets or human beings. For Hobbes, everything works together like a machine.

THE CHARVAKA SCHOOL

The Charvaka school was an ancient Indian philosophy that began in the 6th century BCE. It claimed that the only things that exist are what can be perceived by the senses. For example, this delicious banquet is real because the diners can see, smell, and taste the food.

REALITY IS IN THE MIND

In the 1700s, an Irish philosopher called George Berkeley put forward his theory of idealism, claiming that the world consists solely of things that we can perceive with our minds and senses. This led to the question of whether objects continue to exist if no one actually perceives them.

Is the stone real, or is it just in Johnson's mind?

1 Suppose you're looking at your house. It appears to be real, with everything in the right place.

2 Now imagine that you turn your back on your house. How do you know that it still exists?

3 If reality is just our ideas, what keeps those ideas that make up the house arranged in a certain way?

KICKING A STONE

The English writer Samuel Johnson was a contemporary of Berkeley's and tried to disprove his theory. He famously kicked a stone to show that it was a hard object and not an idea in his mind. But he missed the point—if the stone was just an idea, then the feeling of kicking it could also have been an idea.

WHAT DO YOU THINK?

- At the moment, you're holding and reading this book. You can feel it and see it. Now put the book down and close your eyes. What evidence do you have that the book is still there?

- How can you tell if the world you see around you is the same one that your friends see?

CAN YOU STEP IN THE SAME RIVER TWICE?

Does anything ever stay the same? Change seems to happen around us all the time. Trees shed their leaves, then grow them again, and the sky may cloud over at the end of a sunny day. Does each of the changes we see mean that a "new" thing is created? If not, what does it mean for things to be "the same"? A river consists of water, but because that water is constantly flowing, can you ever step into the same river twice?

1 Imagine that a family is having a day out by a river. While lunch is prepared, the children spend time in the water. The river around them gently flows downstream, and fish swim by.

The fish and all the life in the river are constantly moving..

EVERYTHING IS IN FLUX

The example of stepping into a river twice was first used by ancient Greek philosopher Heraclitus. Some early Greek philosophers saw a complex world that they tried to understand by finding fixed elements—things that stayed the same. Heraclitus, however, described the whole world as being in a "state of flux"—meaning that everything is constantly flowing and altering, like a tree changing with the seasons.

2 As the family has lunch, the river continues to flow. The water and fish that they saw before pass by. The children change, too, as they are now full of food!

3 When the children go back to the river a few hours later, is it the same river? Perhaps the answer lies in how we use language, a view put forward by 20th-century Austrian-British thinker Ludwig Wittgenstein. If a river is defined as "a body of water that is always flowing," there is no longer a problem. The water from before may have flowed on, but it's still the same river.

NEW OR GOOD AS NEW?

When things change over time, do they stay the same or do they become something new? How many changes can be made to something before it becomes entirely different from what it was before? We can look at questions of identity over time with a thought experiment involving the Ship of Theseus.

THESEUS'S SHIP

First recorded by ancient Greek writer Plutarch, this thought experiment opens with the mythical ancient Greek hero Theseus as he returns from his adventures. He is welcomed home by the people of Athens, and they decide to keep his ship in the harbor as a tribute to him.

50 YEARS LATER...

After a bad storm, the ship is left damaged. There are holes in the sail and some oars are broken. It's easy enough to patch up the ship, and soon it looks much like it did before.

60 YEARS LATER...

Years of being in the harbor has caused the ship to rot, so it's given a more significant overhaul. Many of the timbers are replaced with new wood. It looks a little fresher, but is still recognizable as Theseus's ship.

The ship is given some new wooden parts.

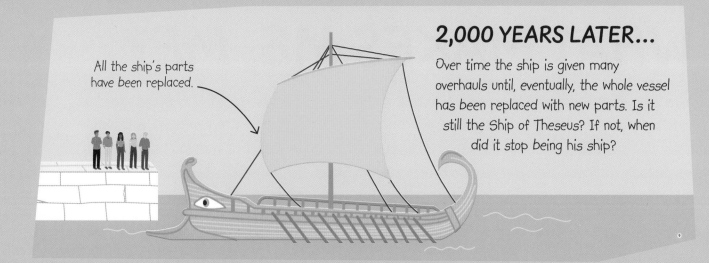

2,000 YEARS LATER...

Over time the ship is given many overhauls until, eventually, the whole vessel has been replaced with new parts. Is it still the Ship of Theseus? If not, when did it stop being his ship?

All the ship's parts have been replaced.

WHICH IS THESEUS'S SHIP?

Taking it further, 17th-century English philosopher Thomas Hobbes imagined that someone had kept all of the old, rotting pieces of the original ship, restored them, and rebuilt the ship from these pieces. Now there are two ships claiming to be the Ship of Theseus—so which is the "real" one?

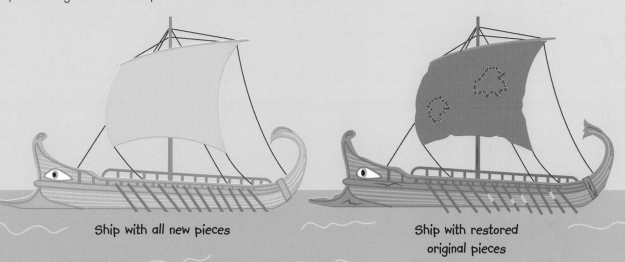

Ship with all new pieces

Ship with restored original pieces

WHAT DO YOU THINK?

- Imagine you have a favorite toy—perhaps a doll or an action figure. One day, one of its arms falls off. Luckily, the toy company sends a replacement arm. Is your toy now a "new" one?

- What if two of its legs fall off and need to be replaced? Or its head? Is it still your original toy? How much of the original needs to remain in order for it still to feel like the same toy?

WHAT MAKES ME, ME?

Have you ever thought about what it is that makes you who you are? Throughout our lives we change a lot. Our hair grows, our baby teeth fall out and are replaced with adult ones, and we get taller. Our likes and dislikes often change, too, but we wouldn't say that we become a "new" person with each of these changes. So do we possess an unchanging thing that means we continue to be the same person now as we were before?

MY BODY IS ME

Imagine you meet an old friend one day and find they've completely changed their look, from their clothes to their hair. You'd still know them as your friend, wouldn't you? Because of all the changes that can happen to our bodies, it must be more than just our physical self that makes us who we are.

The girl's friend has a completely new hairstyle.

Oh wow, you look different!

The girl still knows it is her friend, despite his different appearance.

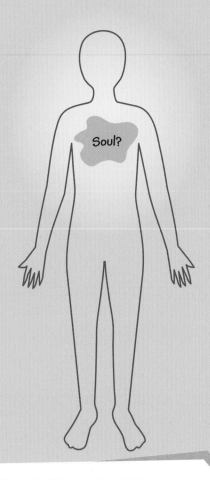

Soul?

I HAVE A SOUL

Some philosophers, such as the ancient Greek thinker Plato, believed every person has a "soul." The soul is separate from the body and lives forever, unchanged over time. These thinkers claim it's the soul that makes you the same person over time, when everything else about you might change.

The cobbler has the prince's memories, so is he the prince?

IT'S ALL ABOUT MEMORIES

The 17th-century English philosopher John Locke thought that our memories give us our identity. He imagined what would happen if the memories of a prince and a cobbler were swapped between their bodies. The person in the cobbler's body would think they were the prince. So according to Locke, that person is the prince.

MEMORY ISN'T RELIABLE

One criticism of Locke's theory is that memory can fail. Suppose someone has been in an accident and has hit their head. They can't remember anything about their life before. But anyone who comes to visit will know exactly who they are. Having the same memories can't therefore be the link between who we were before and who we are now.

The man doesn't recognize himself in the mirror.

1 The 20th-century British thinker Derek Parfit came up with a thought experiment called "The Teletransportation Paradox," in which he imagines a machine that can take all the information about someone and digitally beam it to Mars. In the process, the person on Earth is "deleted."

2 Everything about the person on Earth, including their physical body and their memories, has been recreated on Mars. Is the Mars version the original person transported to a new place, or are they someone new altogether?

COULD THERE BE ANOTHER "ME"?

We may think of ourselves as unique, and that no one else shares the same identity as us. Even in the case of identical twins, their physical appearance may be the same, but they are still two distinct people, each with slightly different personalities, experiences, and memories. But what if there was a way to create a perfect copy of yourself—what would that mean about your identity?

3 The teletransporter has been upgraded and can now create multiple identical versions of the person, without destroying the original. Are these new versions just exact copies of the original person, or individuals in their own right? Parfit concludes that it's impossible to tell.

WHAT DO YOU THINK?

- How different are you now from when you were younger? Have some things stayed the same?

- How would you feel if you came across an identical version of yourself?

THE FUTURE SELF

Parfit thought that your identity remains the same, even though in the future your physical body may be different. He argued that this means you have a duty to look after your future self through how you behave in the present. For example, we know that exercise is good for us, so Parfit claimed that we should follow a healthy lifestyle now in order to give ourselves the best chance of a fit and active old age.

COULD WE EVER TRAVEL THROUGH TIME?

Time travel certainly exists in science-fiction books, TV shows, and movies. Sometimes characters even travel to alternate timelines where they can change things without affecting their own past or future. But if you could travel to a different point in your own timeline, would you be able to change things? Is there even a past or future to change?

HOW DOES TIME WORK?

We experience time as something that moves forward. For example, a slice of cake being eaten ends up as a few crumbs. But does this forward flow of time actually exist? Or is it just how we perceive things? What if time is a jumbled-up mess of different moments?

A slice of cake moving forward in time

A slice of cake if the flow of time doesn't exist

DO THE PAST AND FUTURE EXIST?

Is there even a past or a future that you could travel to in the first place? Or is the present time all there is? Some philosophers believe that events in the past no longer exist, and many think that the future doesn't exist yet. But if the past and future do exist, how do they exist alongside the present?

Eternalists believe that all times exist—the past, present, and future.

Followers of the "growing block" theory say that only the past and present exist.

According to presentists, only the present moment exists.

CAN YOU CHANGE THE PAST?

If time travel does exist, then it raises tricky questions. If you can change the past, you could change it so that you were never born, and you wouldn't be able to travel back in time in the first place. But if you can't change the past, why can't you? What is stopping you from changing things?

1 If time machines existed, you might try to use one to go back to medieval times. But can you do anything there that would change the past?

2 Imagine that on your travels you dueled to the death with an evil knight. If you hadn't traveled back in time, this knight might have lived a long life.

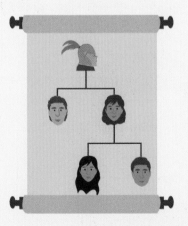

3 What if the evil knight was one of your ancestors? If you killed him, how would you be able to be born to go back in time to defeat him?

WHAT DO YOU THINK?

- Do you think the past exists somewhere other than in our memories? What if people have different memories of the same event?

- If you could go back in time, would you try to change anything? Do you think you would be able to?

- Can you think of any good reasons why we may not have seen any time travelers yet?

WHERE ARE ALL THE TIME TRAVELERS?

If time travel is possible, then why haven't we been visited by time-traveling tourists from the future? The British physicist Stephen Hawking thought this was the best evidence that time travel to the past cannot happen. To test his theory, he held a party for time travelers, but he didn't advertise that it was happening until after it took place. Nobody showed up.

WHY AM I HERE?

What is the point of existence? Does everything and everyone have a particular purpose? For centuries, philosophers have asked these questions and wondered about humanity's place in the universe. Some have said that the point of our existence is to live a life of virtue, while others claim that we discover our purpose by choosing how we want to live our lives.

1 When a person creates an object, they usually have a purpose in mind for that object. For example, a pair of scissors is shaped by its maker to do a specific thing—to cut paper. It makes sense then to say that the scissors' purpose is cutting paper.

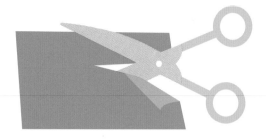

2 Can we say that living things such as plants and animals have a purpose? Were they born to do certain things? Is a honey bee's purpose to collect pollen and make honey? Perhaps it's meant to protect the hive's queen, or to defend the hive's honey from bears.

Thinker:
SIMONE DE BEAUVOIR

Simone de Beauvoir was a 20th-century French philosopher who believed in existentialism—the idea that every person has free will and is responsible for making decisions about their own life. She used existentialism to criticize the unfair and unequal pressures that are placed on women who live in a patriarchal (male-dominated) society.

3 Some philosophers believe human beings are born with a basic purpose that we are driven to fulfill, no matter who we are. The ancient Greek thinker Aristotle believed our purpose was to live a life of virtue. Some people might say our purpose as human beings is to have children and carry on the species.

WHAT DO YOU THINK?

- Is there a purpose you feel you were born with?
- What choices would you make if you were free to do whatever you wanted?

4 Perhaps every person is born with their own unique purpose. But what if someone was born in a society where they were expected to work in an office, even if they didn't enjoy it? Should they stay in that job just because it's what they're supposed to be doing?

5 Can we instead decide what our purpose is? The 20th-century French thinker Jean-Paul Sartre believed that we are free to make choices in our lives that help us discover our purpose. A person working in an office job they don't enjoy has the freedom to decide that their true purpose is to become a firefighter.

Radical freedom

Women are often expected to become mothers and stay at home. What if a woman wanted to become a pilot, but decided in the end to be a stay-at-home mom? De Beauvoir would say the woman should have made her choice entirely based on what she wanted to do—a concept called "radical freedom"—rather than giving in to the pressures of society.

DOES GOD EXIST?

The followers of most religions around the world believe in one or more gods or other divine beings. Is it possible to prove that such beings exist? Many European philosophers, in particular, have sought to prove the existence of the Christian God, giving a number of arguments over the centuries.

THE GREATEST BEING

The 11th-century English archbishop and thinker Anselm of Canterbury believed that God's existence could be proved just by thinking it through. His argument is presented below, though over the years many have pointed out problems with it.

THE FIRST CAUSE

The ancient Greek philosopher Aristotle said that everything that moves has to be set in motion. So the Universe must have been set in motion by an "unmoved mover." Early Christian philosophers argued that this "unmoved mover" is God, who is the cause of the Universe and everything that happens within it.

If God does exist, God would be the greatest being we can imagine.

↓

We can imagine such a being, so God exists at least in the imagination.

↓

Something that exists in reality is greater than something that exists only in the imagination.

↓

So if God only exists in the imagination, we can imagine a being that is greater than God.

↓

But we cannot imagine any being greater than God, therefore God must exist in reality.

THE WORLD DESIGNER

The 18th-century English priest William Paley said that if you look inside a complex bit of machinery, such as a watch, you'll see that the inner workings must have been created and arranged to some kind of design. Paley argued that many things in nature, such as the human eye, are just as complex. The world must have been created by design, and its designer is God.

THE SOURCE OF GOOD

Some thinkers point to the fact that humans are born with a conscience—an instinctive sense of right and wrong—as proof that God exists. They say that the best explanation for why we have this conscience is that it must have come from God.

PASCAL'S WAGER

Rather than trying to prove God's existence, 17th-century French thinker Blaise Pascal thought it was in people's best interests to believe in God. Pascal said that if God and the afterlife don't exist, then nothing bad will happen whether you believe or not. But if God does exist, you will be rewarded for believing or punished for not believing for all eternity. This argument is known as Pascal's Wager. But what if God doesn't punish those who don't believe? Or only rewards believers of a particular religion?

	God exists	God does not exist
Believe in God	Eternal happiness	Nothing
Do not believe in God	Eternal misery	Nothing

THE BURDEN OF PROOF

Sometimes *believers* ask nonbelievers to prove that God doesn't exist. But 20th-century British philosopher Bertrand Russell argued that when people make claims that cannot *be* scientifically disproved, such as "God exists," it's up to them to prove their claim is true. Russell's argument does not directly rule out the existence of God; instead it argues that the *burden* of proof lies with the *believer.*

1 To illustrate his argument, Russell came up with a famous thought experiment. He imagines there is a person who *believes* that there is a china teapot floating in orbit around the Sun, somewhere *between* Earth and Mars. This teapot is too small to be seen by even the most powerful telescopes on Earth.

2 The believer goes on to tell others about the teapot, who doubt its existence and think he is talking nonsense. The believer may *be* offended by their reaction, but he cannot expect others to agree with him just *because* they cannot prove that he's wrong. The doubters don't have to offer any evidence that the teapot doesn't exist.

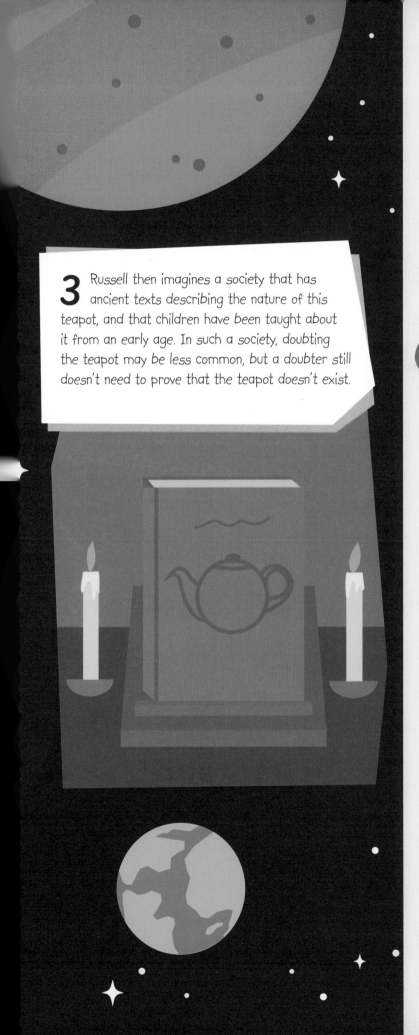

3 Russell then imagines a society that has ancient texts describing the nature of this teapot, and that children have been taught about it from an early age. In such a society, doubting the teapot may be less common, but a doubter still doesn't need to prove that the teapot doesn't exist.

THE NATURE OF GOD

What is God like? Many thinkers have argued that God, if such a being does exist, is far removed from human experience, and therefore unknowable. But 17th-century Dutch philosopher Baruch Spinoza did not *see* God as a remote, mysterious being. For him, God is a part of everything in the Universe, from rocks and trees to animals and humans.

Made in humanity's image

The 19th-century German philosopher Ludwig Feuerbach rejected the Christian belief that humans were made in God's image. He suggested that humans create gods in their own image, projecting our best qualities onto imaginary beings. Feuerbach said that instead of pushing our ideals onto the gods, we should focus on nurturing these qualities within ourselves.

WHY DOES SUFFERING EXIST?

Why do bad things happen to good people? Why does evil exist? Some Eastern religions see suffering as a natural part of life. The philosophy of the Buddhist religion teaches that to be aware of the great suffering that exists in the world is the first step toward spiritual enlightenment. By learning the Four Noble Truths, Buddhists can achieve enlightenment and live without suffering.

THE TRUTH OF SUFFERING

The first Noble Truth, known as *dukkha*, is the knowledge that suffering is universal. Everyone in the world has the capacity to suffer. People do not have to be in great pain to be suffering. A person may just be dissatisfied with their life and feel that everything is an uphill struggle.

THE CAUSE OF SUFFERING

The second Noble Truth is the truth of *samudāya*, which teaches that the source of human suffering comes from our cravings for possessions and other things that we think will make us happy. It is our yearning to fulfill these desires that brings about evil—greed, ignorance, and hatred.

THE PROBLEM OF EVIL

For religions such as Christianity that believe in a benevolent (all-good) and omnipotent (all-powerful) God, how can suffering be explained? Why do natural disasters and diseases happen? In philosophy this is known as the problem of evil. Some Christian thinkers argue that God is not omnipotent but is involved in an ongoing struggle with the Devil, who brings evil into the world.

Buddhism

The religion of Buddhism began in India around the 6th century BCE. According to tradition, it was founded by a prince named Siddhartha Gautama, who gave up his comfortable life to wander as a teacher. He was known as the Buddha.

THE EIGHTFOLD PATH

The last of the Four Noble Truths is *magga*, also known as the Eightfold Path. It is a series of steps that lead toward spiritual enlightenment, or *nirvana*, an awareness that frees a person from the cycle of death and rebirth. It is often represented as a wheel with eight spokes. By following the principles of the Eightfold Path, Buddhists can work toward finding their own inner peace.

THE SOLUTION FOR SUFFERING

The third Noble Truth is called *nirodha*, and it brings an end to our cravings. By detaching ourselves from our desires—by giving them up—we can begin to escape the cycle of suffering.

Right view
Learning and coming to understand Buddhist beliefs.

Right mindfulness
Developing a constant awareness of the mind and the body.

Right intention
A devotion to the path of Buddhism and giving up worldly cravings.

Right concentration
Focusing the mind into a meditation state without distractions.

Right speech
Speaking truthfully and with kindness. Avoiding arguing, lying, and gossiping.

Right effort
Striving to resist feelings of doubt, desire, and ill will toward others.

Right livelihood
Not possessing anything more than is strictly necessary.

Right action
Not performing any act that creates conflict or causes harm to others.

Evil and free will

Some Christian philosophers argue that people can be evil to each other because God gave us free will. Without evil, we wouldn't be able to choose to be good. The 4th-century philosopher Augustine of Hippo said that God didn't create evil, which is just an absence of goodness. People create evil through their actions, so God is not responsible for the existence of evil.

WHAT'S THE POINT OF THINKING ABOUT KNOWLEDGE?

Ideas about what we can know and how we acquire knowledge are central to many aspects of life. For example, the difference between believing something is true and knowing it is true becomes crucial when giving evidence in a court of law. Discussions about the way we learn have helped decide how you are taught at school. And the theory of knowledge that assumes the future will be like the past has enabled scientists to explain how the world works based on observations of previous events.

DO I BELIEVE OR DO I KNOW?

We say things all the time like, "I know my dinner will be on the table when I get home." If you have been told that your meal will be ready for you when you get back from school, then you may have a good reason for thinking this. But it's just a belief—you can't *know* this until you walk through the door and actually see the food there. Your very good reason, or justification, for believing needs to be backed up by the fact or truth. That's what knowledge is—or is it?

1 It's possible to have a justified belief of something that is actually true, but still not actually *know* that thing, because the reason for the belief turns out to be false. Imagine that a farmer counts her sheep at the end of the day and finds that one is missing.

2 The farmer goes to the field to look for the sheep and sees a familiar white shape in the distance. She's relieved to think the sheep is in the field after all.

3 However, what the farmer thinks is her sheep is actually a white bag snagged on a fence. Her belief is justified, and seems to be true—but it's based on false information.

4 The sheep really is in the field, but it's hidden by a large tree. The farmer's belief in the sheep's presence is true *by accident*, and not for the reason she thinks. Did she really *know* the sheep was in the field?

WHAT IS KNOWLEDGE?

Ancient Greek philosopher Plato said that for something to count as knowledge, it must be true, and you must have good reason (justification) for believing it: justified true belief (see right). This theory was accepted for more than 2,000 years, but in the 20th century, US thinker Edmund Gettier pointed out that in certain circumstances, as shown above, knowledge appears to need more than justified true belief. These exceptions to Plato's rule became known as "Gettier cases."

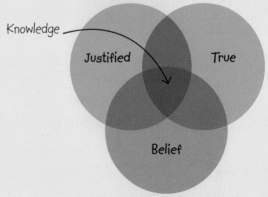

Knowledge

Justified   True

Belief

Plato's definition of knowledge

WHAT DO I KNOW FOR CERTAIN?

Do you ever doubt things that people tell you? What if someone told you that human beings could grow as tall as trees, or that pigs could fly? You might say that's impossible, but some philosophers argue that we can never know anything for certain. So where do we start if we want to gain knowledge?

What does it mean to be a good student?

A good student is someone who works hard at their studies.

But don't some students get good grades without doing much work at all?

Yes, that's certainly true.

Are they bad students?

No, I wouldn't say that.

So being a good student isn't all about working hard, is it?

IT'S IMPOSSIBLE TO KNOW ANYTHING

In ancient Greece, a group of thinkers called the skeptics claimed it was impossible to know anything for sure because even our senses can trick us. Someone lost in a desert might think they have found a small lake, but when they reach it they realize it's a mirage—an optical illusion caused by the bending of light rays. If we can't trust our senses, how can we claim to know anything?

The mirage tricks the girl's senses into seeing a pool of water.

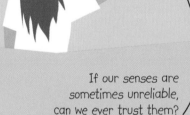

If our senses are sometimes unreliable, can we ever trust them?

With his statement, "I think, therefore I am," Descartes concluded that his ability to doubt was proof of his existence.

YOU CAN KNOW YOUR OWN EXISTENCE

Is it possible to doubt everything, including your own existence? Not according to 17th-century thinker René Descartes. If you can doubt your own existence, then you must exist, otherwise who is doing the doubting?

HOW DO I KNOW I'M NOT DREAMING?

Have you ever wondered if everything around you exists only in your imagination? Suppose that you woke up one morning from a very realistic dream. You might be confused at first, because the dream had seemed so real. But if you cannot tell you are in a dream while you are dreaming, how can you tell that you're not dreaming right now? Daoist philosopher Zhuangzi had just the same thought when he once dreamed he was a butterfly.

In the dream, Zhuangzi believes he is the butterfly.

While dreaming, Zhuangzi is unaware that it's a dream.

1 Zhuangzi returned home one day very tired after working hard. He lay down on his bed and immediately fell into a deep sleep. Zhuangzi soon began to dream that he was a butterfly, fluttering around a beautiful garden.

2 When Zhuangzi woke up, he realized that it was impossible to tell whether he was a man who had dreamed he was a butterfly, or whether he was now a butterfly dreaming he was a man.

Thinker: ZHUANGZI

Zhuangzi lived in China in the late 4th century BCE and was an important thinker in the philosophy of Daoism. He is believed to have written some or most of a Daoist book that is named after him, the *Zhuangzi*, which contains short and amusing stories such as the one featured here.

Daoism

The philosophy of Daoism teaches its followers to accept life's troubles and find joy in everything. The *dao*, or "the way," is the creative force of the Universe, in which all things are united and in balance. Yin and Yang represent this balance.

Yin Yang symbol

Yin represents darkness and things like old age and weakness.

Yang represents light, youth, and strength.

WHAT DO YOU THINK?

- Have you ever had a dream that you woke up from, thinking it had really happened? What made you realize it was a dream?

- When you are dreaming, are there things that make you realize it is not real—for example, flying like a bird?

41

COULD I JUST BE A BRAIN IN A VAT?

How do you know you can trust your own senses? What if your senses are being deceived? And if it's possible that they are being deceived, how do you know that the world around you is really there? Perhaps you are just a brain in a vat, being fed information to fool you into thinking that what you see and hear is real.

2 Now imagine that, in fact, you are not on a beach at all, but simply a brain floating in a vat, hooked up to a complex computer with wires and electrodes.

1 A thought experiment by 20th-century US philosopher Hilary Putnam examines just such a situation. Imagine that you believe you are on a beach, taking in the sun.

3 The computer is stimulating your brain with sensations of being at the beach. It's impossible to tell these sensations from the real thing. Putnam says that if you can't be sure that you're not a brain in a vat, you can't be sure that any of your beliefs about the outside world are true at all.

Thinker:
RENÉ DESCARTES

The 17th-century French philosopher René Descartes wanted to put all of our knowledge on a firm footing. He started from a position of doubting everything, including his senses, and then began to investigate whether there was anything that he could know for certain.

The evil demon
Descartes came up with a thought experiment that is the basis for Putnam's brain in a vat. He wondered if there was an evil demon controlling his senses, tricking him into believing the world around him was real. Descartes concluded that in this situation, the one thing he could be sure of was his own existence.

WHAT IS A CHAIR?

When you think of a chair, what do you see? Perhaps it's something to sit on. It might have a back and four legs. What about other kinds of chairs, like office chairs, rocking chairs, or armchairs? How do we know that something is a chair, if there are so many different types?

Office chair   Rocking chair

Four-legged chair

WHEN IS A CHAIR NOT A CHAIR?

IF I TAKE PART OF A CHAIR AWAY, IS IT STILL A CHAIR?

Perhaps we can come closer to agreeing what a chair is by seeing how much we can take away from it before it stops being a chair. Does this help us identify what all chairs have in common?

Is it a chair if it has no back?

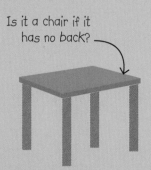

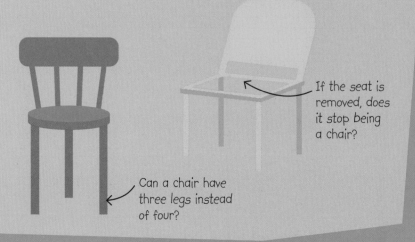

If the seat is removed, does it stop being a chair?

Can a chair have three legs instead of four?

WHY AREN'T OTHER THINGS WE SIT ON CALLED CHAIRS?

There are many other things we sit on, including benches, beanbags, and stools. Why aren't these things we sit on called chairs? Do these examples of "not chairs" help us get closer to what we all understand a chair to be?

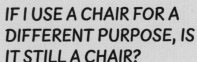

How do we know what a chair is when we see one? What makes a chair a chair? Is it what it's made from? Is it how it's put together? One of the reasons philosophers ask questions like this about simple objects is to highlight the assumptions we make about what we think we know.

IF I USE A CHAIR FOR A DIFFERENT PURPOSE, IS IT STILL A CHAIR?

Is an object's purpose a part of its definition, or not? If a chair is meant to be used for sitting, does it stop being a chair if someone uses it for a different purpose, such as standing on it to hang decorations?

WOULD SOMEONE FROM ANOTHER PLANET KNOW WHAT A CHAIR IS?

Would a chair's definition and purpose be obvious to someone who had never seen a chair before? What if chairs on an alien's planet looked completely different? Would they be confused by the form our chairs take?

HOW DO WE LEARN?

Where does knowledge come from? This question has divided philosophers since ancient times. Some thinkers, called rationalists, argue that we have innate knowledge—we are born knowing things—or that we can work things out using our minds. Others, called empiricists, claim that we learn everything through experience.

LEARNING IS REMEMBERING

The ancient Greek rationalist Socrates once talked to a boy about a geometry problem. The boy knew nothing about math, but by watching Socrates draw diagrams in the sand, he was able to find the answer. Socrates said the boy could "remember" what he already knew by thinking it through.

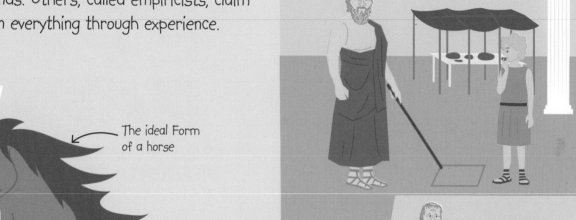

The boy was born with the knowledge to solve the puzzle.

The ideal Form of a horse

PLATO'S THEORY OF FORMS

The ancient Greek philosopher Plato claimed that there is a world of Forms—perfect versions of everything that exists in our world. We are born knowing these Forms, so that whenever we see a horse, we recognize it as a horse because we know the ideal Form of it.

The real-world horse reminds us of the perfect Form of a horse.

EXPERIENCE TELLS US EVERYTHING

Plato's pupil, Aristotle, disagreed with his teacher and claimed that we learn everything through experience. Aristotle tried to make sense of what he saw in the world around him by grouping things together based on features they had in common. For example, all birds have a beak, feathers, and talons, so we can recognize birds from these features.

Bird

- ✓ Beak
- ✓ Feathers
- ✓ Talons

Thinker:
PLATO

The 4th-century BCE Greek philosopher known as Plato was a student of the great thinker Socrates. Many of Plato's works record the real or imagined conversations, or dialogues, between Socrates and other philosophers. Because of this, it's hard to know which are Plato's ideas and which are his teacher's. When it comes to theories of knowledge, both were rationalists.

THE GREAT DEBATE

The disagreement between Plato and Aristotle about where knowledge comes from led to a great debate between rationalists and empiricists in Europe that lasted for many centuries, and many of the greatest thinkers in history put forward their arguments to support one side or the other. Eventually, 18th-century German thinker Immanuel Kant came up with a theory of knowledge that combined elements from both traditions.

DOUBTING DESCARTES

The 17th-century French rationalist René Descartes realized that sometimes our senses give us a false impression, so we can't trust our experiences. The things that we can know for certain, such as the fact that we exist, can be known through reasoning.

A pencil in a glass of water appears bent, so our senses can't always be trusted.

THE BLANK SLATE

The 17th-century English empiricist John Locke suggested that the mind is like a blank slate when we are born, with nothing written on it. Only through having experiences of the world do we start to fill our minds with knowledge, and this process continues throughout the rest of our lives.

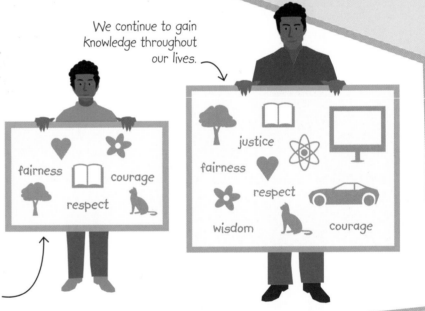

We continue to gain knowledge throughout our lives.

justice
fairness
respect
wisdom
courage

fairness
courage
respect

As we grow, our minds get filled with more and more knowledge.

HUME'S PINEAPPLE

According to 18th-century Scottish empiricist David Hume, "We cannot form to ourselves a just idea of the taste of a pineapple, without having actually tasted it." It's only by having the experience of eating a pineapple that we know how it tastes.

EXPERIENCE AND INTUITIONS

Immanuel Kant argued that we can only know the world as it's experienced by our bodies. We can't get out of our bodies to check whether what we experience matches the world as it actually is. But Kant also believed that we are born with some knowledge, which he called intuitions, to help us make sense of our experiences. For instance, our intuitions of space and time allow us to understand objects and how they behave over time.

Intuitions in our minds, such as space and time, allow us to make sense of our experiences.

We can't know anything about how things actually are in the world.

We can only know about our experiences of the world.

TWO TYPES OF TRUTH

The 17th-century German philosopher Gottfried Leibniz said that there were two kinds of truth: truths of reason and truths of fact. We can tell that truths of reason must be true just by thinking about them. Truths in mathematics such as 2+2=4 are truths of reason. Truths of fact can't be verified just by thinking about them; we have to check them against reality.

"A triangle has three sides" is a truth of reason.

"The Great Pyramid of Giza is in Egypt" is a truth of fact.

WHAT CAN EXPERIENCES TELL ME?

You may think you can learn all about some things, such as how aircraft fly, by reading books or learning about them at school. But when you see or experience something for the first time, do you learn anything more than if you just read the facts about it? The contemporary Australian philosopher Frank Jackson thinks that you do, and came up with the thought experiment known as "Mary's Room" to explain his idea.

Mary herself exists in black and white.

Information about light waves helps Mary understand how color works.

1 Mary has lived all her life in a black-and-white room. She is a scientist who specializes in how we see color, and she knows how light is processed by the brain so that we perceive different colors. However, Mary has never seen color herself.

2 One day, Mary finally leaves her room and *sees* color for the first time. Does she learn anything new? Jackson claims that she does. While Mary knew the physical properties of color, she wasn't aware of certain things that are associated with them—how colors make you feel, for example. Therefore, it's not possible to learn everything without experience.

Mary learns new things about color that her coworkers have always known from experience.

1 The 19th-century US pragmatist William James asked what would happen if you were lost in a forest and came across a path. Whether you remain lost depends on what you *believe* about the path.

Do you believe the path will lead you deeper into the forest or to safety?

DO BELIEFS NEED TO BE TRUE?

Does it matter whether we can prove that a belief is true? Or is the belief's usefulness more important? Suppose that there are two possibilities: either diamonds are always hard, or they are soft until they are touched. The truth of either theory makes no practical difference. Some philosophers, called pragmatists, say this shows that something only needs to be "true" so long as it has a practical application in our lives.

2 If you do not know or believe that the path will lead out of the forest, and so do not follow the path, you will continue to remain lost in the forest. Your action of staying where you are has made your *belief* true.

3 If you instead *believe* that following the path will lead you out of the forest and to safety, that idea will cause you to take an action—follow the path—which will eventually get you out of the forest and also make your *belief* true. James would prefer this belief because it's useful.

WHAT DO YOU THINK?

- Have you ever changed your mind about something you *believed* to be true?

- Have you ever made something you *believe* true by acting as though it is?

- What's the difference between a belief and a fact?

PRACTICAL BELIEFS

Sometimes having a *belief* is useful because it spurs us to do good things. Someone's belief in God might lead them to do charitable acts such as helping hand out blankets to homeless people.

Education

John Dewey, a 20th-century US philosopher, believed that philosophy should be used to find practical solutions in people's lives. He was particularly interested in revamping education. He thought students would learn more easily if they could actively participate. For example, instead of only learning the theory of chemistry, students should have the opportunity to participate in science experiments.

IS SCIENCE ALWAYS RIGHT?

The Sun has risen every day since humans can remember, and science suggests that it will continue to do so. But can we really say that the Sun will definitely rise tomorrow? Science is based on a process of thinking called induction. This uses past events to predict the future, and assumes that nature will always behave in the same way.

1 The 18th-century Scottish thinker David Hume said that science is based on assumptions that may not be correct. We have no real reason to believe that the Sun will rise tomorrow.

Thinker
FRANCIS BACON

The 16th-century English philosopher and politician Francis Bacon proposed a new method to test scientific hypotheses, which used induction to analyze the results of experiments. His process formed the basis of the modern scientific method.

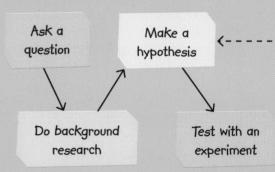

Ask a question

Make a hypothesis

Do background research

Test with an experiment

2 Hume said that we have no proof that the laws of nature will not change, we just assume they will remain the same because they have done so in the past. So it is possible that the Sun will not rise tomorrow.

3 Using induction—acting as if things will continue as they've always done—is an important tool in daily life. But induction relies on a circular argument to prove itself true: the future will behave like the past because it always has. In other words, we use induction to prove induction.

The future will behave like the past.

Why do we think it will continue to do so?

Because it has done so before.

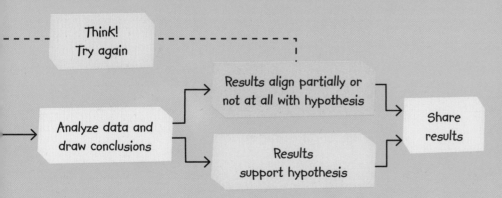

Think! Try again

Analyze data and draw conclusions

Results align partially or not at all with hypothesis

Results support hypothesis

Share results

The scientific method
Science is based on testing hypotheses, which are assumptions that scientists use as a starting point for their theories. These hypotheses are tested through experimentation and observation. If the tests support the hypotheses, scientists share their theories.

MISTAKES MOVE SCIENCE FORWARD

The problem of induction troubled scientists for more than a century until a 20th-century Austrian-British philosopher, Karl Popper, suggested a different way to approach science. Popper said that science is concerned with proving theories false, rather than proving them to be true.

1 A scientific theory starts with an assumption known as a hypothesis, such as "all swans are white." This hypothesis is used as a starting point for scientific testing and observation.

2 The hypothesis that all swans are white remains useful to science as long as every swan observed by scientists or reported to them continues to be white.

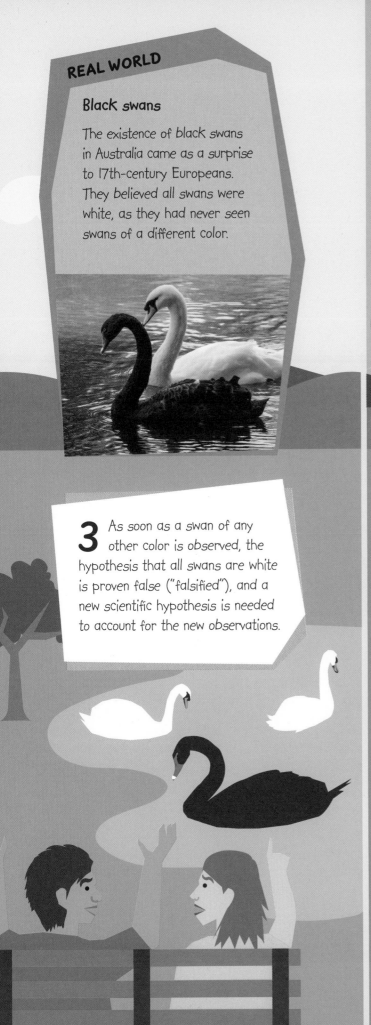

Black swans

The existence of black swans in Australia came as a surprise to 17th-century Europeans. They believed all swans were white, as they had never seen swans of a different color.

3 As soon as a swan of any other color is observed, the hypothesis that all swans are white is proven false ("falsified"), and a new scientific hypothesis is needed to account for the new observations.

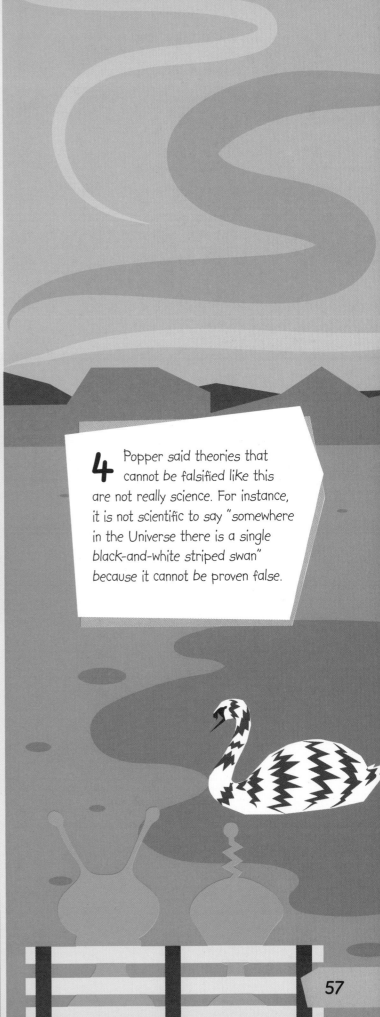

4 Popper said theories that cannot be falsified like this are not really science. For instance, it is not scientific to say "somewhere in the Universe there is a single black-and-white striped swan" because it cannot be proven false.

WHAT'S THE POINT OF THINKING ABOUT
RIGHT AND WRONG?

Deciding what the right thing to do is can be a challenge, but luckily we have philosophy to guide us. This area of thought is called moral philosophy or ethics. It can help us decide what kind of person we want to be and how to lead a happy life. These decisions are closely related to questions about whether we are truly free to choose what we do and if there should be limits to our freedom. Attempts to answer these questions have become the basis of many laws and customs around the world today.

CAN AN ACT ITSELF BE GOOD OR BAD?

Is it possible to tell if an act is right or wrong by itself—without considering the reasons behind it? Can you say that certain acts are by definition "good" or "bad"? For example, is donating to charity always a good act, and is it always bad to steal money from someone?

Does it matter if this man has reasons for taking money? Is stealing always wrong?

HOW CAN I TELL RIGHT FROM WRONG?

DO YOUR INTENTIONS MATTER?

If you act with good intentions but the consequences are bad, are you in the wrong? For example, if you decide to be generous and share a cookie with a friend without realizing they are allergic to one of the ingredients, does that mean you did a bad thing?

IS DOING THE RIGHT THING DOING WHAT YOU'RE TOLD?

Is it right to obey someone just because they are in charge? What if a boss told their employee to do something that is wrong, such as shredding documents that could prove the boss guilty of a crime? Would it be wrong for the employer to challenge the boss if they think what they are being told to do is wrong?

It's not always easy to know the right way to act or behave. Sometimes you might think you are doing the right thing, only for it to lead to the worst consequences. So how can we tell right from wrong?

WHAT IF EVERYONE ELSE IS DOING IT?

Sometimes it feels that behaving a certain way must be acceptable because everyone else is doing it. But imagine that you are surrounded by people who are all jumping off a cliff. Would you do it, too?

CULTURAL DIFFERENCES

Some things are considered right in some cultures but wrong in others. For example, it is common for people in the US and Europe to eat beef. However, for followers of the Hindu religion in India, cows are believed to be divine creatures, and are highly respected. Killing them for their meat is unacceptable behavior.

In many parts of India, cows are protected as sacred animals.

IS IT EVER RIGHT TO TELL A LIE?

Have you ever been told that lying is always wrong? Perhaps you don't agree—maybe you can think of a time when you needed to lie to spare someone's feelings, or to get out of trouble. But does having a good reason make it okay to lie? What would happen if everyone lied all the time? Would you be upset if you found out that your parents or your friends had lied to you?

1 Imagine your friend gave you a gift on your birthday but it was exactly the same as a gift you'd already been given. Would you be honest with them, or would you tell a "white" lie to protect their feelings?

2 Lies often lead to more lies. If another friend knew you already had the present, would you ask them to lie for you and hide the original? You might have to get many people involved to protect your lie.

You have had to ask another friend to go along with the lie.

IMMANUEL KANT

Immanuel Kant was a 17th-century German thinker, and his ideas on what makes actions right and wrong remain influential. Kant said that there are certain principles that everyone must follow. If some people follow these principles but others don't, it makes the principles useless.

3 If you told your friend the truth from the start, they might feel bad for getting you a gift you already had, but it would prevent you from getting caught up in a web of lies. The philosopher Immanuel Kant said we must always tell the truth, otherwise everything is chaos.

You have decided to tell your friend the truth, even if it might upset them.

Sticking to principles
According to Kant, people should never act outside these principles, even for good reason. For example, a prison guard might believe one of her inmates to be innocent and want to let them out of prison. But if she did let them out, and other prison guards started to do this, too, there would be no order and the law would be meaningless.

IS IT PART OF YOUR RELIGION TO BE GOOD?

Almost all religions tell us that we shouldn't do bad things, such as stealing, and instead do good deeds, such as giving money to people who are less fortunate. Many people believe that when they die, God will punish or reward them for the things they did in their lives.

SHOULD I BE GOOD?

IF YOU WERE INVISIBLE, WOULD YOU STILL BE GOOD?

The ancient Greek philosopher Plato thought that people only stop themselves from doing bad things because they know they will be punished. But what if you were able to turn invisible? You could rob a bank and no one would ever know. Is this something you would do if you had the chance? Is it just the fact that you might be caught that stops you from doing bad things?

WHAT IS "GOOD," ANYWAY?

What makes something good or bad? For example, this girl is playing with her cat, and she is not doing her homework. But what if looking after the cat is one of her responsibilities? The 18th-century Scottish thinker David Hume said that there's nothing to say whether something is good or bad—it depends on our own opinion or feeling.

We are often told that we should be good and that it is wrong to behave badly. But why should we be good? What do we get out of good behavior? Sometimes being bad is more fun, or gets us what we want—so what stops us from behaving badly?

WHAT DO YOU THINK?

- How do you define good behavior? Is your definition the same as your parents' or teachers' definition?

- When you do something good, how do you feel if no one notices?

- Do you think it's okay to do bad things if no one will know?

IF YOU DO THE RIGHT THING AND NO ONE NOTICES, IS IT WORTH IT?

Do we do good things because we will be rewarded, or is doing good its own reward? The ancient Greek philosopher Aristotle said people who have virtue do the right thing for the right reason. But what is the right reason? Do you return a lost dog because you'll get a reward, or because it's the right thing to do?

Reward
$100

DO THE ENDS JUSTIFY THE MEANS?

Suppose you break a promise to meet a friend. We'd normally say this was the wrong thing to do. But what if you broke your promise so you could visit your sick grandmother in the hospital—would failing to meet your friend now be a "good" thing? Judging the consequences of our behavior rather than what we actually do is one way of deciding what's right and wrong. It means we consider that the ends (the results of our actions) justify the means (the way we go about them).

ANY MEANS NECESSARY

The thinker Machiavelli believed that people in charge had a duty to use any means to get good results. Imagine that a sports team manager is forced to drop a player who is loved by the fans to improve the team's dynamics. The next time the team plays, they win the game. Machiavelli would say that firing the player was the right thing to do.

GREATEST HAPPINESS

The 18th-century British thinker Jeremy Bentham focused on the outcome rather than the intention of an act. He thought that the way to judge what's right is to measure what creates the greatest happiness for the greatest number of people. This is known as the Principle of Utility.

THE HARM PRINCIPLE

John Stuart Mill, a 19th-century British thinker, saw that the Principle of Utility might restrict some people's freedom. He introduced the Principle of Harm: you can do what you like in order to achieve the greatest happiness for yourself as long as it doesn't hurt other people.

One person is helped when the man takes his neighbor a plate of food.

Many people are helped when he volunteers at a soup kitchen.

The boy can't concentrate on his book because his sister's video game is too loud.

When the girl is wearing headphones, both of them can enjoy their hobbies.

Thinker:
NICCOLÒ MACHIAVELLI

In the 1500s, an Italian political thinker called Niccolò Machiavelli wrote a book called *The Prince*, in which he argued that the ends do justify the means. He discussed how people in power should be allowed to do immoral things, such as be violent or deceitful, if it resulted in a better society for all.

TO DO OR NOT TO DO?

If we rely on the results of our actions to tell us what's right or wrong, we can create situations that feel wrong no matter what we do. The 20th-century British philosopher Philippa Foot's thought experiment "The Trolley Problem," about a runaway trolley (train), shows how looking for the best outcome can lead us to behave in a way we'd normally think was wrong.

1 In our version of Foot's thought experiment, a runaway train is heading toward five people doing maintenance work on the track. They haven't noticed the approaching train, and without intervention they will die.

2 A man is standing next to a lever that could divert the train to a second track, saving the five workers. However, there is one worker on that track who would be killed instead. What, if anything, should the man do?

The lever changes the switches on the track to divert the train.

3 Philosophers known as utilitarians would say that we should create the greatest happiness for the greatest number of people. So the man should pull the lever, because it will mean that fewer people will be harmed.

Is this person's life worth less than the lives of the other five?

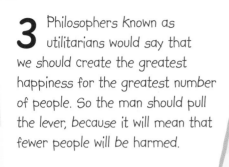

TAKING IT FURTHER

Suppose the man was standing next to a woman on a bridge over the runaway train's track. If the man pushed her off the bridge, her body would stop the train from reaching the five workers. Would actively pushing someone to their death be any different from pulling a lever?

This person will die if pushed off the bridge.

4 Saving the five workers might be the best outcome in utilitarian philosophy, but if killing people is wrong, why is doing something that results in a person's death the "right" thing to do here? It seems that focusing on the outcomes of our actions doesn't always help us.

WHAT IS HAPPINESS?

Little things, like getting a present, or spending time with a friend, can make you happy. But the happiness these events bring often goes away quickly. What's the secret of long-lasting happiness? According to the ancient Greeks, it's all about living a good life. But they had many different ideas about what counts as a good life, and how to achieve it.

NEEDING NOTHING

Socrates said that everyone naturally wants to be happy, and happiness is teachable and can be worked at. He thought that to be truly happy, we should learn how to act wisely rather than focus on gathering possessions. According to a story by his student Plato, one day Socrates walked through the marketplace and said, "Look at all these things I don't need."

SELF-CONTROL

Plato thought that only people who behave well can be happy. He pointed out the importance of self-control, and of not doing anything to excess.

A SIMPLE LIFE

A group known as the Cynics believed that happiness can be found when you reject luxury and wealth, as well as the customs of society. The famous Cynic Diogenes took this to the extreme, living in a ceramic jar in the marketplace of Athens.

Diogenes saw that a dog has nothing, and is happy to do as it pleases.

PLEASURE

The Hedonists believed in a life of pleasure. However, the famous Hedonist Epicurus said that our behavior needs to be governed by prudence (cautious decisions). He defined happiness as the absence of suffering.

Epicurus lived on a diet of bread and water, as he didn't believe in eating to excess.

WHAT DO YOU THINK?

- What makes you happy? A nice meal, spending time with your friends, receiving presents? Do you need to keep having these experiences to be happy?

- Think about the things you have but don't need. Would you be less happy without them?

- Does your happiness depend on things or experiences, or is it something deeper within yourself?

ACCEPTANCE

Another group called the Stoics believed that life always involves some suffering. We need to come to terms with that fact, and let go of feelings of fear and frustration. We can then lead a good and fulfilling life, in harmony with nature.

THE LEGEND OF DIOGENES AND ALEXANDER THE GREAT

When Alexander the Great heard of Diogenes, he visited him on the streets to ask if he could help. Diogenes is supposed to have responded, "Yes, you can step aside because you're blocking the Sun." This story shows that Diogenes had not only identified life's essentials (such as sunlight), but rejected power and authority, too.

IT'S ALL IN THE BALANCE

Another ancient Greek philosopher, Aristotle, thought that happiness was being the best that you can be. Aristotle's idea of a good, happy life was based on "virtues," moral qualities such as courage, kindness, patience, and generosity. Aristotle considered too much or too little of these qualities to be a bad thing.

1 Every virtue has two extremes: too little (a deficiency) and too much (an excess). Take the example of generosity. Suppose someone is lucky enough to win the lottery, and they are deciding what to do with their fortune.

$1,000,000

2 Our lottery winner might be stingy about the money, and give just a tiny portion of the prize to some of his friends. For Aristotle, meanness is not being generous enough, and being mean will not bring you happiness.

Thinker: ARISTOTLE

The 4th-century BCE Greek philosopher Aristotle studied under Plato, but he had very different ideas. He wrote more than 200 books, including *Nicomachean Ethics*, which tried to show people how to live a good life. According to Aristotle, it's not enough to know what a good life is, the important thing is to live it, and become a good person.

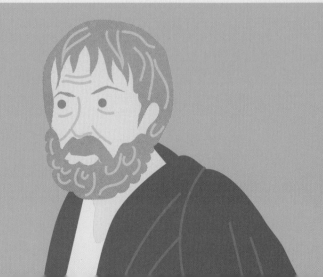

Lots of the money is going to waste.

3 Suppose the lottery winner decides to give away a lot of the money without really thinking about it. Aristotle would consider this type of generosity excessive. According to him, living to excess is also no way to live a good life.

4 To be truly generous—the best at giving you can be—you must find the middle ground between deficiency and excess. But who's to say what the perfect balance is? Of course, every circumstance is different, so we need to judge each case individually.

WHAT DO YOU THINK?

- Let's take another virtue: patience. Have you ever behaved impatiently? Or with so much patience that people took advantage of you?

- If so, what could you have done to achieve a better balance?

- Do you think the balance is different for each person?

The Golden Mean

According to Aristotle, acting virtuously means finding the balance between two extremes—he called this tipping point the "Golden Mean." For example, if we want to act courageously, we have to find the middle ground between being reckless (having too much courage) and behaving like a coward (not having enough courage). We have to learn what this balance is for each virtue.

Recklessness   Courage   Cowardice

UNHAPPY HUMAN OR HAPPY PIG?

You may have heard the phrase "ignorance is bliss," meaning that we can be happy if we are unaware of unpleasant situations. But is this true? The idea that a happy existence is filled with pleasure and free from worries is known as hedonism, and it's been around since the times of ancient Greece. It sounds like hedonism could give us the perfect life, but is there more to happiness than this?

1 The 19th-century British philosopher John Stuart Mill said that endless pleasure makes humans no different from animals. Both can enjoy a life free from troubles. However, people have the ability to think—what philosophers call "the power of reason." For Mill, it's what makes a human life more meaningful than an animal's life.

Market

The woman is bathing happily, choosing to ignore disaster outside.

The pig is happy, unaware that it will soon be sold for food.

2 You might prefer to be out having a good time with your friends instead of studying. But think about how rewarding it might be to use hard "brainwork" to achieve your goals. Is it worth sacrificing enjoyable outings with your friends to work toward greater happiness in the future?

The boy is finding his study hard and isn't very happy.

3 Suppose that passing your exams led to the job of your dreams in the future. You might end up being much happier as a result. Mill thought that the quality of our happiness is better than the quantity of it. It's always better to be a temporarily unhappy human who is working toward a rewarding outcome than to be blissfully ignorant like the pig.

The boy's hard work paid off and he is now happier than he was before.

WHAT DO YOU THINK?

- Do you think you would be truly happy if you chose to ignore all the problems in the world?

- What's your favorite thing to do? Is it a purely physical pleasure, such as eating a meal, or does it involve using your brain in some way?

- Do you think there are different levels of happiness?

- Do you feel a greater sense of reward when you succeed at something after you've worked hard?

HIGHER AND LOWER PLEASURES

John Stuart Mill thought that there were different kinds of pleasures. He put them into two categories: higher and lower. A higher pleasure is an activity that uses brain power. Reading a book takes more brain power than watching TV, so it is the "higher" pleasure and watching TV is the "lower" pleasure. Mill claimed that higher pleasures are better because although they are more demanding, they are often more rewarding.

Watching TV is often less demanding than reading.

Reading requires "brainwork," but could be more rewarding.

THE AMAZING EXPERIENCE MACHINE

Is it right to judge the value of our experiences by how happy they make us? Robert Nozick, a 20th-century US philosopher, didn't think so. His thought experiment, "The Amazing Experience Machine," aims to show that people would choose real life—even if it means having some negative experiences—over an artificial life of only amazing experiences.

You could choose the experience of adopting a cute animal.

You might want to buy a cool car.

Perhaps you would enjoy having the experience of hugging your family.

1 What if you could hook up to a machine that stimulated your brain to give you only good experiences? You could choose any situation you like, but once attached to the machine, you wouldn't know it wasn't real life. Would you choose a virtual life over reality?

You could choose the experience of winning a race.

2 Would winning a race in real life feel better than winning in the machine? You would have run the race, rather than just had the experience of winning. Nozick argued that people actually want to do things, so they would not choose the Amazing Experience Machine over real life.

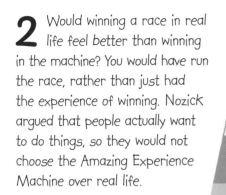

REAL WORLD

Virtual reality

People can now play games and visit places they haven't been to in real life by using virtual reality devices. The experiences that these devices offer are fun, but would you want to be hooked up to them your whole life?

WHAT DO YOU THINK?

- What have you accomplished in your life that has made you feel good?

- Did the path to achieving your accomplishments give you pleasure?

- If your accomplishments took place in a virtual world, would you still feel as if you achieved something?

AM I FREE?

When we make a choice, are we really free to choose whatever we want, or are the decisions we make shaped by outside forces? If we are not free to do whatever we want, does that mean that we cannot be held responsible for our actions? Some philosophers argue that we are free to make our own choices at all times, while others believe that freedom of choice is an illusion.

YES, I'M FREE

According to some philosophers, we have free will, which means we can choose to act as we wish. The 20th-century French thinker Jean-Paul Sartre said that it doesn't matter what our circumstances are, we are always free to choose how to respond to our environment.

I CAN DO WHATEVER I WANT

Imagine you're a musician in a trio, and you're supposed to go to practice. The other members of the trio might be counting on you to be there, but if you have free will, you always have the freedom to decide not to turn up.

I'M RESPONSIBLE FOR MY ACTIONS

Sartre says that because you have free will, you are responsible for your actions. If your fellow musicians ask you to leave the group for missing practice, you must bear responsibility for this outcome because you had the option to make a different choice.

Law and freedom

Most legal systems around the world are based on the philosophy that people have free will and are responsible for their actions. This means they must bear the consequences and can be made to pay fines or serve time in jail.

NO, I'M NOT FREE

Some thinkers say that we are not free and everything is predetermined, or chosen for us, by our circumstances. These philosophers are known as determinists. The 17th-century Dutch determinist Baruch Spinoza said that free will is an illusion, and all of our choices are decided for us.

I HAVE NO CHOICE

What if you were supposed to get up for school, but instead slept in? If you don't have free will, philosophers who believe in determinism would say that this event was completely out of your control. You didn't have a choice because it was predetermined that you would miss school.

AM I RESPONSIBLE FOR MY ACTIONS?

If you miss school, it's likely that you'll be punished and have to go to detention. But if everything is predetermined and it wasn't your choice to miss school, should you have to deal with the consequences of your actions? According to philosophers such as Spinoza, you don't have free will, so you aren't responsible for your actions.

AM I A HAPPY PRISONER?

Most of the time, it feels like we're free to make our own choices. We can choose our friends, or refuse to eat our vegetables at dinner. But what if, for some reason, the choice to do the opposite wasn't available to us? Some philosophers argue that we are free only if we could have made a different decision.

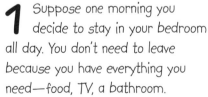

1 Suppose one morning you decide to stay in your bedroom all day. You don't need to leave because you have everything you need—food, TV, a bathroom.

2 What you don't realize is that your door has jammed and won't open. Even if you wanted to leave, you wouldn't be able to. So is your choice to stay in the room still a real choice?

WHAT DO YOU THINK?

- What things are you not allowed to do? Is there a good reason why? Who or what is stopping you?

- Do you think being able to choose makes you truly free?

- What is the one thing you wish you could do but can't? Swim like a fish? Travel back in time?

Thinker:
JOHN LOCKE

The 17th-century English philosopher John Locke was also a politician. He was interested in the relationship between an individual's freedom and the role of government. He thought that society should protect people's "natural rights": life, liberty, and property (belongings).

Voluntary choice

Locke saw a difference between voluntary actions and being physically free to do something. We might want to grow wings and fly, but we can't change the laws of nature! Locke concluded that, although we may have free will, we don't always have liberty.

SHOULD I BE ABLE TO SAY WHATEVER I WANT?

Nobody can stop you thinking whatever you like, but what if you wanted to speak your thoughts out loud? Should we be able to say anything that comes into our minds, even if it offends other people? Many countries have laws that protect free speech, and some have laws that make certain speech, such as hate-speech, a crime.

SHOULD FREE SPEECH ALWAYS BE ALLOWED?

What if we were allowed to say anything we wanted, no matter if it was offensive or led to violence or crime? Imagine someone told other people they should vandalize a billboard, but that person didn't take part in the crime. The crime happened because of their speech, so should they be punished along with the others?

SHOULD WE BAN FREE SPEECH?

Should we ban certain kinds of speech in order to stop people from causing offense? If so, where would we draw the line? Different things are hurtful to different people. If all offensive speech was banned, a dog owner who was offended by someone saying they didn't like dogs might be able to have that person arrested. Is that fair?

This person is openly telling people to commit acts of vandalism.

Should you have the right to stop someone from expressing their opinion?

At what point should offending somebody be considered a criminal offense?

DOWN WITH DOGS!

IS CENSORSHIP OKAY?

If we start to ban speech, this could lead to censorship. This is when people in power prevent access to books, films, or other media they think is inappropriate, such as violent movies for kids. But who gets to decide what should be censored? Could it be taken too far? What if a political leader was able to ban newspapers and websites that disagreed with their views?

Should governments be allowed to censor online content?

WHAT DO YOU THINK?

- Do you think people should be able to say things you don't agree with?

- Have you ever said something you believe in strongly, but that someone else found offensive? How would you feel if you were banned from saying it again?

Thinker:
JOHN STUART MILL

John Stuart Mill was a 19th-century British philosopher who believed that people should be free to pursue their own happiness, as long as it didn't prevent the happiness of others. He was a strong supporter of women's voting rights, argued against slavery, and defended the right to free speech.

Free speech

Mill believed that free speech was necessary for society to progress and grow. In many countries, people exercise their right to free speech by protesting and going on marches for causes they care about, or against ones they don't agree with.

WHAT'S THE POINT OF THINKING ABOUT
EQUALITY?

People all over the world live in groups, or societies. Since the earliest times, philosophers have debated the best way to organize society, discussing issues such as whether laws can protect our rights and how we can treat people fairly or equally. Theories about equality can guide us to behave in a way that doesn't hurt others and can help us identify where people's rights are being taken away. Recently, philosophers have thought about how equal right can be extended to animals and our place in the environment as a whole.

HOW SHOULD WE TREAT OTHERS?

Just because someone is different from you, does that mean they should be treated differently? The 20th-century French thinker Simone de Beauvoir said that when we think of what we are, we often also think of what we are not, which de Beauvoir called "the Other." In many societies, people who are seen as the Other often face discrimination such as racism, sexism, or ableism.

1 What if a population of aliens came to Earth and humans now had to share the planet with them? The aliens are very different from the humans, but they are also not identical to each other. What if the humans start to define themselves as "not alien" and see the aliens as Other? How do you think the aliens would be treated?

This alien has been denied a high-paying job because it isn't a human.

2 The humans have become the dominant group, and they control the opportunities that the aliens have. Sometimes enough people with similar characteristics get together and become more powerful than other groups. They can then deny opportunities to people they see as Other.

3 The humans may offer some opportunities to the aliens who reject all or parts of their own culture to try to fit in with human society. Sometimes the dominant group tries to erase the qualities and differences of other groups by either encouraging or forcing them to adopt the dominant group's customs.

The alien is adopting human dress customs because it will give it better opportunities.

In this *baseball* game, the humans and aliens play the *best* position for their individual skills.

4 What if the humans accepted and appreciated the qualities that the aliens have? The 20th-century French philosopher Emmanuel Lévinas said that instead of "othering" people *because* of their differences, we should acknowledge and celebrate those differences since they are what make us all unique.

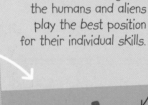

WHAT DO YOU THINK?

- Do you compare yourself to other people to define who you are or who you are not?
- How do you treat people who are not like you?
- Have you seen or experienced examples of Othering?

SHOULD WE TREAT EVERYONE THE SAME?

With billions of people in the world, each with their own individual needs, how can we make sure that everyone is treated equally? What exactly does equality mean? Some people might say that if everyone is given the same tools, that makes things equal. But does that make it fair? What if each person needs different tools to be successful and achieve the same goals?

1 Does equality mean everyone should have access to the same tools? In an equal world, everyone at a supermarket would be given the same-sized stool to reach items on the top shelf. But the child and the wheelchair user still can't reach.

This man is tall enough to reach the top shelf. He doesn't need to use the stool.

Even with a stool, the child is too short to reach the top shelf.

A stool is of no use to the wheelchair user.

2 What if everyone was given tools particular to their needs? A taller stool for the child and a ramp for the wheelchair user mean that everyone can reach the higher shelf. Giving different people different tools based on their needs is known as equity, and it means that everyone has access to the same opportunities.

3 If the shelves are lowered, these people don't need a stool or a ramp and they're able to reach the items on the shelves without assistance—the barrier of height has been taken away. Everyone is being treated the same, but all people's needs are taken into account.

Thinker:
MARY WOLLSTONECRAFT

Throughout most of recorded history, women have been seen as inferior to men. In the 1700s, English writer and philosopher Mary Wollstonecraft challenged this idea, and was one of the first women to promote equal rights between men and women.

Women's suffrage

Wollstonecraft was a passionate supporter of women's rights. She was one of the first people to argue that women should have the right to vote. Her ideas helped inspire the women's suffrage movement in the late 1800s.

DO WE NEED A STRONG LEADER?

Thomas Hobbes, a 17th-century English thinker, thought that people are selfish and violent by nature. Without laws—and a strong leader to uphold the laws—people would do what they wanted with no regard for the welfare of others. Hobbes believed that this would lead to chaos and disorder.

SHOULD WE ELECT OUR LEADERS?

According to 17th-century English philosopher John Locke, it should be up to the people to decide who governs them and who has the power to create and uphold laws. In many countries today, this decision is made through democratic elections.

In a democracy, people vote to decide who will have the power to lead them and make laws.

WHO SHOULD HAVE POWER?

Would you choose to live in a completely free world with no rules or structure, or would you prefer to live in a society governed by a leader? In societies, we give up certain freedoms in exchange for other benefits, such as safety and security. The leaders in a society create laws that we agree to obey to ensure such things as protection from harm and a basic standard of living. But how do we decide who should have the power to make those laws?

SHOULD WE GOVERN OURSELVES?

In the 1700s, French thinker Jean-Jacques Rousseau argued that people are good by nature and that civilized society prevents them from living freely. According to him, rulers make laws to protect their property, rather than for the good of the people. He suggested that people should have direct control of the government so that they could make laws based on their "general will" (common interests).

In the 18th century, Rousseau's ideas inspired the leaders of the French Revolution to overthrow the monarchy.

WHAT DO YOU THINK?

- Do you think people could live alongside each other in peace if there were no rules or laws to force them to behave in a certain way?

- Are there benefits to living in a society that is run by laws and government?

- How would you set up a society that functioned in a way that was good for everyone?

Thinker: CONFUCIUS

Confucius was a Chinese philosopher born in 551 BCE. He was a dedicated student and eventually rose up to become Minister for Justice for his home state of Lu. He traveled around China to spread his ideas and taught that people at every level of society should act with virtue and sincerity.

Leading by example

Rather than simply giving orders and telling people what to do, Confucius said that rulers should lead by example. For example, a good ruler who cares about protecting the environment might help plant trees with his subjects.

This king is planting trees to encourage others to do the same.

SHOULD WE MAKE THINGS FAIR?

Some people in the world have a lot and are very fortunate, while many are very poor and struggle to survive. If we had the power to change the world, would we give ourselves the best opportunities over others? Or would we make things fair for everyone? What if we didn't know what we were going to get in advance?

1 On a smaller scale, imagine it is your job to choose between two plays for your class to perform. You really want to get a major role with lots of lines, but your teacher won't be revealing what part you're going to play until after you've chosen.

2 The first play has only one lead part. If you choose this script, it is likely that another classmate will get the starring role, while you end up with a small chorus part. Would you risk getting a small part for the slim chance of getting the lead?

It's more likely you'll get a small part if you choose the first play.

3 All of the parts in the second play have a similar amount of lines and time on stage. If you choose the second play, you and your classmates will all get small but equal parts. Would you be happy to have an equal share of the spotlight with everyone else?

Everyone gets an equal part in the second play.

WHAT DO YOU THINK?

- Do you think everyone should have the same chances and opportunities in life?

- Do you think things are currently fair for everyone? Can you think of times when things aren't fair?

- If it were up to you, how would you make things fair for everyone?

THE VEIL OF IGNORANCE

The scenario shown above is based on a thought experiment made popular by 20th-century US philosopher John Rawls, called the "Veil of Ignorance." Rawls argued that if we had the power to build a world and had no idea about our social standing and abilities before we were in it, we'd be more likely to choose an equal division of wealth and opportunities.

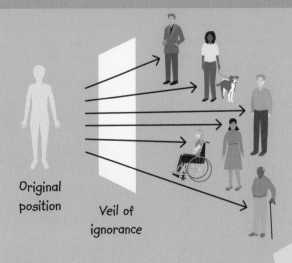

Original position

Veil of ignorance

SHOULD I GIVE TO CHARITY?

We probably think that it's a good idea to give to charity, but with so many people in need, how do we decide who to help and when we've done enough? These concerns have been called the "expanding circle" of charity and were discussed by the contemporary Australian philosopher Peter Singer in a thought experiment about a drowning person.

1 In this version of Singer's thought experiment, a girl goes into a shoe store to buy a new pair of sneakers. She's saved up for a long while to afford them, and she's really proud to have the latest design.

The man is drowning and there's no one else to help.

2 On her way home, the girl spots a man in danger in a river. She could easily throw him a life preserver to save him from drowning, but in order to get to it, she will have to risk getting her brand new sneakers dirty.

3 Singer claims that most people would think a human life is more valuable than sneakers and decide that they had a duty to save the man, as long as they didn't put themselves in danger.

The girl's sneakers are now ruined by the mud.

4 Singer argues that if we have a duty to help someone close to us, then surely we should also help those who are farther away, perhaps even in another part of the world. But where does this "expanding circle" of charity stop?

It's easy for the girl to help someone who is close by.

A boy on the other side of the world is equally in need of help.

REAL WORLD

Effective change
Charity is often about giving people access to the things they need, rather than just donating money. In areas where clean water is limited, installing a pump can be the most effective way to help people.

SHOULD WE TREAT ANIMALS AS EQUALS?

Over the past century, there has been a dramatic shift in the way we think about our relationship with animals. At the heart of this shift is the question of whether animals deserve the opportunity to live their lives freely, without us interfering. So should animals have the same rights as humans? And if not, what rights should they have?

BIOLOGICAL MACHINES

In the past, humans were seen as different from and superior to animals. The 17th-century French philosopher René Descartes considered animals to be inferior biological machines. But in the 1800s, advances in biology showed that humans were just another type of animal, and attitudes began to change.

ANIMAL RIGHTS VS. HUMAN RIGHTS

Some philosophers argue that it is acceptable to harm an animal if that would prevent it from hurting a human. Animals may have rights, but humans also have a right to health and safety. So how far do the rights of humans outweigh the rights of animals?

Is it okay to test human medical cures on animals?

ARE ALL ANIMALS EQUAL?

Many people get upset when harm is done to cats, dogs, or other mammals. But most people wouldn't mind exterminating cockroaches. Philosophers have argued that mammals, birds, and some other animals have conscious minds, while others such as insects may be more like biological machines. But no one as yet has agreed on which animals can suffer.

A cat lover may think nothing of swatting a fly.

DO ANIMALS HAVE RIGHTS AT ALL?

Some philosophers disagree that animals have rights. One argument put forward for this view is that rights come with an understanding of duty—how we should behave toward others. A tiger doesn't understand that it is wrong to kill, so it shouldn't have any rights.

SHOULD ANIMALS BE FREE?

Do we have a duty to protect animals, even if it means they are not free? Is the safety offered to a pet better than the freedom it would have in the wild? Is it right to keep animals in zoos? Some animals might otherwise become extinct. For example, pandas kept in captivity are safer than pandas that are free in the wild, where they are exposed to poachers. So should we keep them safe?

WHY SAVE ENDANGERED SPECIES?

When a species of animal is in danger of becoming extinct, we try to save it by protecting its habitat and reducing human interference. But we still farm animals for their meat and other products. Why do we prioritize one life over another? For example, why is the life of a panda or a tiger more important than that of the farm animals we eat?

WHAT DO YOU THINK?

- If you have a pet, do you treat it better than other animals?

- Is it right to test products like make-up on animals?

- Is it okay to wear animal fur? What about leather shoes?

- Is an animal's life in captivity better than a life in the dangers of the wild?

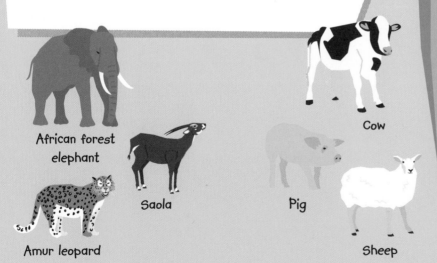

African forest elephant

Saola

Cow

Pig

Amur leopard

Sheep

IS IT OKAY TO EAT MEAT?

Many people around the world don't eat meat for a number of different reasons, such as for their health or because of religious beliefs. But for moral vegetarians, eating meat is just plain wrong. The philosopher Peter Singer argues that animals have the capacity to suffer, and it is the suffering inflicted on livestock animals that makes people turn to vegetarianism.

1 Singer believes that it's wrong to inflict unnecessary suffering on a conscious being. Animals can experience pain similarly to humans. The farming and killing of animals for meat and other products cause animals to suffer. There are alternatives to eating meat, so eating meat that comes from such farming is wrong.

Free-range farming
Animal products such as eggs might be marketed as free-range, meaning that the animals that produce them are not kept in a cage. But how much freedom these animals have varies significantly. Some free-range animals suffer just as much as their caged counterparts.

2 Singer's argument in favor of vegetarianism also supports veganism—the practice of not eating any animal products, including eggs or milk. Animals that are farmed for these products suffer, too. For example, cows in the dairy industry often end up developing painful medical conditions.

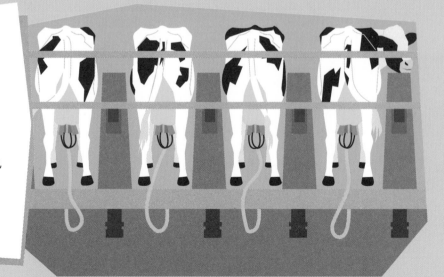

3 Some philosophers who disagree with Singer point out that eating meat can give great pleasure to many humans, and this pleasure outweighs the harm that is done to animals. Others say that many farm animals wouldn't exist if everyone stopped eating meat. But is a life of suffering that ends in being eaten better than not existing at all?

4 A different argument against eating meat looks at its environmental impact. Animal farming does much more damage to the environment than crop farming. For example, animal waste and gases contribute to global warming. So is it right to farm animals when there are less harmful alternatives?

Forests are cut down to make room for animals to graze.

Vast amounts of water are used for farm animals.

Animals produce huge amounts of methane, a greenhouse gas that causes pollution.

Thinker: PETER SINGER

The contemporary Australian philosopher Peter Singer is a leading figure in the fight for animal rights. He argues that when it comes to suffering, animals are our equals. So if we are to do the least amount of harm, we must consider the effect our actions will have not just on people but also on animals.

Speciesism

Singer's term "speciesism" describes the attitude of treating humans as more important than animals. He predicts that people in the future will look back on our treatment of animals with disgust and will view speciesism in the same way that sexism and racism are viewed today.

WHY DOES THE ENVIRONMENT MATTER?

Until the late 19th century, humans saw themselves as existing apart from nature. They believed they were superior to all other things, which existed only as resources for humans to use. Many people believe that the environmental issues we face today are a result of this human-first mindset. But does the environment matter? And why?

HUMANS ARE SUPERIOR

The view that nature exists to serve humans is not as widespread as it once was, but some people still believe it today. Most of these people take a more long-term view than people in the past. They want to protect the environment so that humans can continue to exist.

"THINK LIKE A MOUNTAIN"

The 20th-century US philosopher Aldo Leopold said that we should "think like a mountain." We should appreciate how animals, plants, and habitats are all interconnected. If you change just one thing, it can have an impact on a whole ecosystem.

DEEP ECOLOGY

The root cause of environmental problems lies within human nature itself according to deep ecologists such as 20th-century Norwegian philosopher Arne Naess. Deep ecology proposes a new way for humans to relate to nature.

1 All human and nonhuman life has value, and the diversity of life forms is part of this value. Humans have no right to reduce this diversity except to satisfy essential human needs.

2 Humans have already interfered with nature to a critical level, and interference is worsening. Human and nonhuman life cannot continue to flourish if this interference continues.

Deforestation not only affects plant life but also destroys animal habitats.

3 Governments must shift away from systems that damage the environment. We should focus on a good quality of life instead of increasing our wealth and comfort.

Cities should be built in harmony with their surroundings.

WHAT'S THE POINT OF THINKING ABOUT
THINKING?

We often talk about thinking as something that happens in our minds, but it's not always clear what a mind is and whether it's something different from a brain. Philosophical questions about the mind are important in subjects such as psychology and neuroscience, as well as in developing artificial intelligence. Philosophy can also make us better at thinking things through, helping us to create good arguments and recognize bad ones.

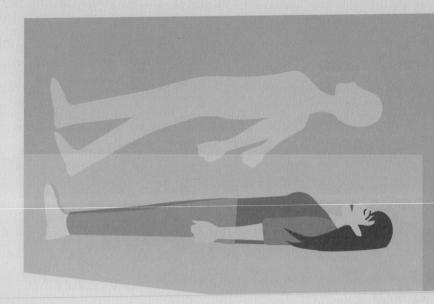

IS THE MIND THE SOUL?

The idea of a mind is a fairly modern one. The ancient Greek philosopher Plato thought that something called the psyche, or soul, is what animates our bodies. He believed the soul to be indestructible and immortal. Plato's idea became central to many religions.

WHAT IS A MIND?

As human beings we think and feel, make calculations, have hopes and fears, experience the world through our senses, and store memories of these sensations. We say that these activities happen in the mind. But what exactly is a mind?

IS MY MIND IN MY BRAIN?

Many philosophers have looked to the brain for an explanation of the mind. Rather than considering the mind to be something separate from the part of our body that does the thinking, they say that the mind relates to the brain and is a physical thing that cannot exist without the body.

IS THE MIND SOMETHING WE DO?

Perhaps thinking of the mind as a "thing" is a mistake. Perhaps instead it's something that we "do." A group of 20th-century philosophers known as behaviorists believed that all mental activity can be reduced to behavior. They saw the mind as a collection of behaviors that we perform, rather than a thing that exists in itself.

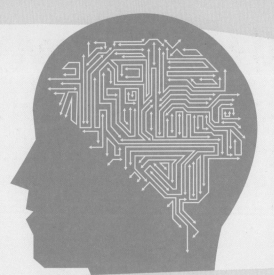

IS THE MIND A STREAM?

What is in our minds is always changing. Our attention might shift from a sensation, to a memory, and back again. Perhaps the mind can be seen as a process, a flowing "stream" of mental activity in which thoughts appear and disappear.

DOES THE MIND EVEN EXIST AT ALL?

Some modern thinkers say that things we think of as happening in the mind don't really exist at all. Our thoughts and ideas are just the results of chemical interactions taking place within the brain.

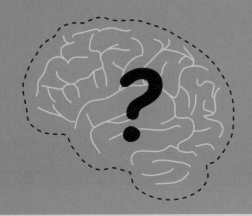

REAL WORLD

Neuroscience
The scientific study of the brain is known as neuroscience. It explains how the brain behaves when we have experiences, but it may never be able to examine what having these experiences feels like.

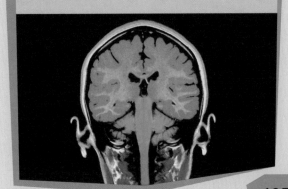

WHERE IS MY MIND?

Where are our thoughts, feelings, and memories located? We use our brains to think and feel, but thoughts aren't physical objects in the brain, at least not in the same way that a car or this book is a physical object. But if the mental contents of the mind are not part of the physical world, then where does the mind exist?

THE FLOATING HUMAN

The 11th-century Islamic philosopher Ibn Sina thought that a person's mind (or "soul" as he knew it) was separate from the body. In a thought experiment, he imagined a person floating in empty space, with no information from their senses about the outside world or their own body. Ibn Sina said that this person would still think of themselves as "me," even though they couldn't link this "me" to a physical body.

FROM MIND TO BODY

If mental activity is separate from the body, how do we go from having the thought "I want to kick this football" to the body taking action and kicking the ball? This question has puzzled philosophers for centuries and is known as the Mind–Body Problem.

GHOST IN THE MACHINE

The 20th-century British philosopher Gilbert Ryle rejected the idea that the mind is separate from the body. Ryle said that what we call "mind" is nothing beyond the functions of the brain, so to say that the mind controls the body is like imagining some kind of "ghost in the machine."

WHAT'S IT LIKE TO BE A BAT?

This question was asked by 20th-century US philosopher Robert Nozick. No matter how much we learn about the brain of a bat, said Nozick, we'll never know what it actually feels like to be a bat soaring through the air. So that feeling must exist outside the processes of the bat's brain.

MENTAL PROPERTIES

One theory about the mind's relationship to the body is that the brain has two types of property. It has physical properties, such as having a wrinkled surface, but it also has mental properties, such as having experiences. This theory is known as property dualism.

Size

Shape

Color

Emotions

Sensations

Memories

WHY FEEL AT ALL?

The contemporary Australian philosopher David Chalmers has pointed out that wherever the mind exists, this still doesn't explain why the mind has experiences in the first place. What is the point of feeling pain when you stub your toe? Why does a scent bloom in your mind when you smell flowers?

WHAT DO YOU THINK?

- Is your mind a part of your body?

- If you lost a part of your body, does that mean that you would lose a part of your mind?

- If you were able to construct a set of wings that let you fly, would the feeling of flying with them be the same feeling a bat has in flight?

CAN I KNOW WHAT YOU'RE THINKING?

Can we ever really know what somebody else is thinking and feeling? Or that they think in the same way that we do? Or even that they are thinking at all? We might assume that others think and feel like we do because their behavior is similar to our own. But we have no real way of knowing what is going on inside. This is known in philosophy as the "problem of other minds."

1 When you are happy, you might smile. So when you see a person smiling, it makes sense to assume that they are happy. Your belief about what they are feeling is based on their behavior.

"I'm happy!"

"I'm sad, but I don't want my friend to know."

2 But it's possible that the person is smiling to hide other feelings—they might be pretending. So behavior is not always a good indication of what others are feeling or thinking.

3 If behavior cannot give us a true picture of what somebody else is thinking and feeling, is it possible to know that they are thinking at all?

PHILOSOPHICAL ZOMBIES

The contemporary Australian philosopher David Chalmers imagined the existence of "philosophical zombies." These beings look and behave like normal people, but they do not think at all—there is nothing going on inside.

We can't see into other people's minds, so how can we be sure that they are not philosophical zombies?

4 Imagine a red object. Is there any way to know whether the red you experience is the same red that another person experiences? It's possible that you or the other person might be color-blind, but even if not, it's impossible to get into their mind to find out if your experiences are the same.

You   Another person

5 For the 20th-century Austrian-British philosopher Ludwig Wittgenstein, language offers a way of thinking about the problem of other minds. Objects that are red must have something in common for us to agree on what the word "red" means. Similarly, language relies on other people in order to work, which suggests that other thinking people exist in the world.

WHAT DO YOU THINK?

- How do you work out how other people feel? Is it by observing their behavior?

- If a person says "ouch," how can you really know if they are in pain?

- Could a robot pretend to have a mind?

You   Another person

CAN A MACHINE THINK?

Will computers ever become so advanced that they could think in the same way humans do? Science fiction has many examples of robots and machines that behave like people. And as technology improves, engineers are able to build more complex machines. So will machines in the future have emotions and act without being instructed? Some thinkers believe they will.

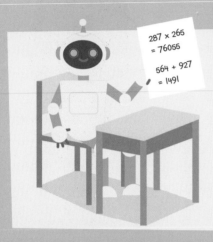

287 × 265
= 76055

564 + 927
= 1491

ARE MACHINES INTELLIGENT?

A group of 20th-century philosophers known as functionalists argued that it doesn't matter how a machine is made, it's the machine's function that is important. They see a machine's intelligence—its ability to do math, for example—as a function. If a machine can perform intelligently, then according to functionalists it is intelligent.

THE TURING TEST

The British computer scientist Alan Turing devised a test in the 1950s to show that a machine could be said to think under certain circumstances. The test measures whether a computer shows intelligent behavior. If the machine can fool somebody into believing it is human, then it passes the test.

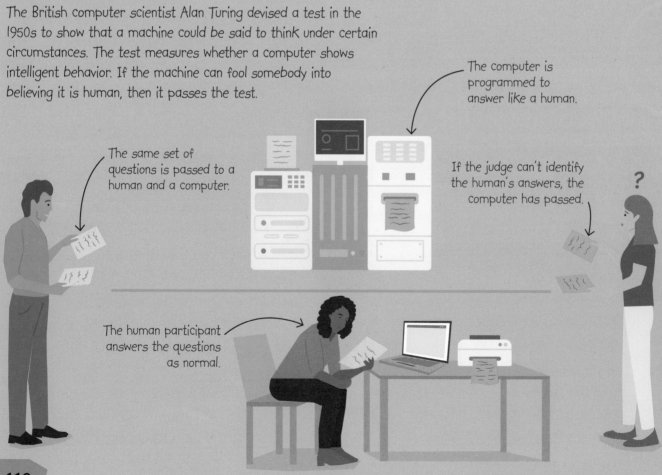

The computer is programmed to answer like a human.

The same set of questions is passed to a human and a computer.

If the judge can't identify the human's answers, the computer has passed.

The human participant answers the questions as normal.

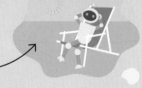

Is it possible for machines to daydream in the same way as humans do?

WEAK AND STRONG AI

Artificial intelligence (AI)—intelligence demonstrated by machines—is sometimes talked about as being weak or strong. Weak AI can be programmed to behave like a human and already exists in modern technology, such as home assistants. But some thinkers argue that strong AI, a machine with a mind of its own, could exist in the future.

WHAT MAKES US DIFFERENT?

It might be difficult to believe that a machine with a mind is possible. But why? Is it because machines are built by humans, and it's impossible to build something that has a mind? Humans are "built" by biology, chemistry, and evolution. If machines can't have dreams and an inner life, then why can we?

ROBOT BRAINS

Functionalists argue that if mental activity is just a function of the brain, it can happen in a brain that is made from different materials from ours. If in the future we were able to build a mechanical brain that works exactly the same way as a human brain, would it be able to think like humans do?

WHAT DO YOU THINK?

- Do you believe that computers will someday have the same kind of intelligence as humans?

- Could a brain made of metal and wires have a mind?

- If a machine acts as if it understands, does it matter whether it actually does?

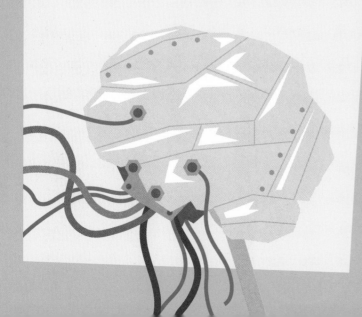

DOES A ROBOT UNDERSTAND?

The idea of computers that can think is exciting, but if such machines existed, what would really be going on inside them? Could an artificial intelligence created by humans really be said to understand or be conscious? Many have argued that while a machine can look like it's thinking, there's no way that it could actually have any understanding.

1 The contemporary US philosopher Daniel Dennett argued that if we say a computer is "intelligent," it's because we don't know how it's been programmed. We can't say that a computer "knows" how to play chess once we understand its programming.

A robot playing chess follows a set of programmed instructions.

2 In "The Chinese Room," a thought experiment by contemporary US thinker John Searle, a person sits at a desk answering questions in a language that they don't speak, read, or understand by using a rule book. The person represents the central processing unit of a computer, and the rule book is its programming. The experiment aims to show that a computer has no real understanding.

This person passes questions in Chinese to the person in the room.

A person reading the answers would assume the person inside understands Chinese.

The person answers the questions in Chinese using the book.

3 One objection to "The Chinese Room" is that if the person was taken out of the room, they could learn the meaning of Chinese words by being in the real world. So perhaps a robot that is able to interact with the world would be able to learn the meanings of its input and output.

REAL WORLD

A learning robot
First activated in 2016, Sophia is a robot designed to improve over time by analyzing its conversations with humans. Sophia gives the illusion of understanding, reacting with facial expressions and a set of preprogrammed responses.

WHAT DO WORDS MEAN?

When you say the word "dog," what exactly does that mean? How do words relate to things? Is the meaning of a word the object that it refers to? Do words even have meanings? You might assume the answer is "yes" to this last question, but many thinkers who have studied the philosophy of language over the past century have argued otherwise.

WORDS ARE SIGNS

Early philosophers of language argued that words themselves don't have meanings. Words are more like signs—they represent a thing or an idea. These signs point to objects or ideas if you learn the connection. If you don't know a language, then you can't understand how its words connect to objects and ideas.

"Dog"

"Dog" =

REAL WORLD

International signs
Sometimes we need information quickly, and without having to know a particular language. To locate exits in an emergency, we have developed internationally recognized signs that people can understand without language.

PICTURING THE WORLD

According to Wittgenstein in his early writings, the purpose of language is to picture the world, which is made up of facts. Language behaves like a camera, allowing us to communicate these facts about the world. Wittgenstein said that statements that don't picture the world—that contain opinions or judgments—have no meaning. They try to say things that cannot be put into words.

The cat sits on the mat.

The cat is a good cat.

Wittgenstein said if you can't picture a statement, it is "meaningless."

LANGUAGE GAMES

In his later writing, Wittgenstein said that the meaning of language is found in how it is used. He said that we play games with language, and we need to know the rules the speaker is using. If a person yells out "Water!" the meaning varies depending on the situation.

LANGUAGE IS SOCIAL

Imagine that a person who speaks a language you don't know says "gavagai," pointing to a rabbit. Even if you rule out other meanings, such as "mammal" or "dinner," you wouldn't know whether "rabbit" was exactly right; "gavagai" might mean "a collection of rabbit parts." According to 20th-century US philosopher Willard Van Orman Quine, this doesn't matter, so long as you can both use the word to communicate.

Thinker:
LUDWIG WITTGENSTEIN

The studies of 20th-century Austrian-British philosopher Ludwig Wittgenstein on words and meaning changed the way we think about language. In his earlier writing, he developed a picture theory of meaning. But years later, he rejected this earlier work and instead described his view of language as a tool for communication.

Family resemblance

Some words, such as the word "game," have a variety of meanings. But no single meaning can explain the link between all the things we call games. Wittgenstein said that there is a "family resemblance" between these meanings. Things that we call games share overlapping similarities of meaning with each other.

WHAT MAKES A GOOD ARGUMENT?

An argument in philosophy isn't a quarrel. It's a series of statements a person makes and the conclusion that follows from them. These statements, which are called premises, should all lead toward the conclusion. A person makes an argument either to prove that the conclusion is true or to prove that it is likely to be true. But what makes one argument better than another?

DEDUCTIVE ARGUMENTS

If someone is attempting to prove that the conclusion to an argument must be true, then they are making a deductive argument. A good deductive argument must be valid (the conclusion follows from the premises) and sound (it's valid and the premises are true).

Premises are statements that support a conclusion.

The conclusion must follow from the premises.

In a deductive argument that is valid, the conclusion must be true if all of the premises turn out to be true. However, the premises don't have to be true for an argument to be valid.

All dogs are mammals.

+

All dachshunds are dogs.

= All dachshunds are mammals.

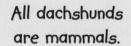

A valid argument in which all the premises are true is a sound argument. An argument is unsound either because it is not valid (the conclusion doesn't follow from the premises) or at least one premise isn't true.

Pigs are animals.

+

All animals can fly.

= Pigs can fly.

This premise is not true, so the argument cannot be sound.

The argument is still valid, as the conclusion follows from the premises.

ERRORS IN DEDUCTION

It's important to structure deductive arguments properly. Some arguments can appear at first glance to be valid, but their conclusions are not necessarily true if all the premises are true. These arguments contain fallacies—examples of faulty reasoning.

If the girl has a twin, then she has a brother or a sister.

+

The girl doesn't have a twin.

= Therefore the girl doesn't have a brother or sister.

The conclusion follows from the "inverse" (opposite) of the first premise, "If the girl doesn't have a twin, then she has no brother or sister," rather than the premise given.

If it rained this morning, the streets would be wet.

+

The streets are wet.

= Therefore, it must have rained this morning.

The conclusion here is reached by "forming the converse" (swapping around the terms) of the first premise to read: "If the streets are wet then it rained this morning." But there may be other reasons why the streets are wet.

INDUCTIVE ARGUMENTS

If someone is attempting to prove that the conclusion to an argument is likely to be true, then they are making an inductive argument. Scientists use inductive arguments all the time—if repeated experiments have led to the same results, it is likely that the next experiment will have the same results, too. Inductive arguments can't be valid, but they can be strong or weak.

Whenever I have looked out on a clear night, I have seen a starry sky.

+

Tonight will be a clear night.

= Tonight I will see a starry sky.

The premises offer strong evidence that the conclusion is true.

I have met two cats in the past.

+

Every cat I have met has disliked me.

= The next cat I meet will dislike me.

This argument is weak, as it relies on evidence from only two encounters with cats.

RECOGNIZING BAD ARGUMENTS

Some types of bad argument get repeated so often that they have been grouped together and given names. These examples of faulty reasoning are known as fallacies, and some of the most common fallacies are explained below. When somebody uses a fallacy, it's not always a genuine mistake in their thinking. Sometimes people make bad arguments intentionally, to convince people of their point of view.

ATTACKING THE PERSON

When someone argues against a person's ideas by attacking their appearance or character, they may be committing an *ad hominem* (Latin for "attacking the person") fallacy. "How can we believe anything you say when you're wearing that outfit" is an *ad hominem* argument.

SLIPPERY SLOPE

The "slippery slope" fallacy involves saying that one thing will lead to a much worse thing when there isn't a strong link between the two. An example would be a student saying: "If I fail a test tomorrow then I will probably fail the whole year, and I'll never be able to get a good job."

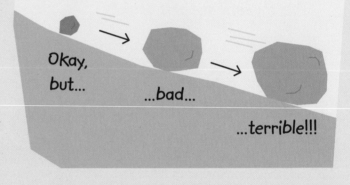

Okay, but...   ...bad...   ...terrible!!!

STRAW MAN

Sometimes a person will alter their opponent's argument and fight against that. For instance, a teenager might say, "You want me to study instead of going out with my friends? Why do you hate my friends so much?" This type of fallacy is known as "attacking a straw man."

Defeating a straw man doesn't defeat a person's actual argument.

FALSE DILEMMA

"We can either go to the cinema or go out for a meal." This is an example of a false dilemma. The speaker is presenting just two choices, but there are other alternatives—staying in, for instance. Sometimes presenting a false dilemma can be helpful, particularly if there are too many options.

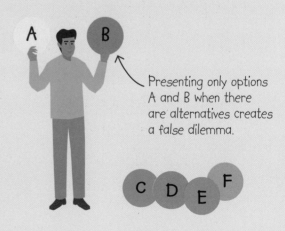

Presenting only options A and B when there are alternatives creates a false dilemma.

AFTER THE EVENT

Sometimes one event is mistakenly given as the cause of a later event. This is known as a *post hoc* (Latin for "after the event") fallacy. A rooster starts crowing long before sunrise, but it would be a *post hoc* fallacy to say that the rooster's crowing causes the sunrise to occur.

APPEAL TO AUTHORITY

Whenever somebody calls on an expert to help convince you of their argument, they might be committing a fallacy known as an "appeal to authority." Does the expert actually know anything about the subject in question? Is there any reason they would be biased? It's always a good idea to investigate the link between the expert and the argument being presented.

If a scientist works for a particular company, can you trust what they say about that company?

PARADOXES

Sometimes an argument leads to a contradiction or appears to go against common sense, but it's difficult to say exactly what has gone wrong. These arguments are known as paradoxes. The ancient Greek philosopher Zeno of Elea came up with many paradoxes. For instance, he pointed out that at any given instant, an arrow in flight is in a particular position—it isn't moving. So how can the arrow be moving at all?

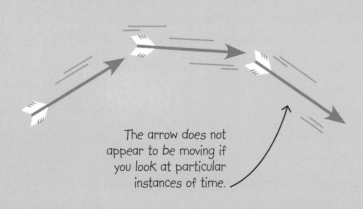

The arrow does not appear to be moving if you look at particular instances of time.

A HISTORY OF PHILOSOPHERS

From investigating the what the universe is made of instructing people on how to lead a good life, philosophers have, since ancient times, strived to uncover the truth about the world and our existence. The people in this timeline are just some of the philosophers whose work has influenced how we think today.

THALES

Nothing survives of this Greek philosopher's work, but we know from others who wrote about him that he was one of the first to ask, "What is the cosmos made of?" According to him, it was water.

c.624–c.548 BCE

DEMOCRITUS

Studying the building blocks of the universe, this Greek philosopher was one of the first to suppose that everything is made up of unbreakable materials, which he called atoms.

c.460–c.370 BCE

SOCRATES

We know about this Greek philosopher through his student Plato. Socrates challenged the views of others through debate and his method of questioning, which we know today as the Socratic method.

c.470–399 BCE

PLATO

The Greek philosopher Plato founded the Academy, the first university-like institution for great minds to debate. His ideas on existence, knowledge, the mind, and society became central to Western thinking.

c.429–347 BCE

ARISTOTLE

Greek thinker Aristotle pioneered the technique of using physical evidence to develop his theories, rather than simply reasoning. He wrote more than 200 books during his lifetime.

384–322 BCE

SIDDHARTHA GAUTAMA

Buddhist legend says this South Asian philosopher became spiritually enlightened while meditating under a sacred fig tree—the Bodhi Tree. He became known as the Buddha and taught people how to avoid suffering.

c.563–c.483 BCE

CONFUCIUS

The Chinese thinker Confucius spent most of his life traveling around what is now modern-day China, teaching people how to be virtuous and respectful toward one another. His ideas have had a lasting impact on Chinese society.

551–479 BCE

PARMENIDES

In his quest to uncover the physical nature of the universe, Greek thinker Parmenides argued that it was impossible for nothing to exist. Therefore, everything is eternal and unchanging.

DIOTIMA OF MANTINEA

Appearing in the works of other philosophers, Greek thinker Diotima debated on matters of love. For her, the meaning of love is to seek out inspiration and beauty.

c.515 BCE

5th century BCE

ZHUANGZI

Best known for his tale of dreaming that he was a butterfly, Chinese thinker Zhuangzi wrote light-hearted stories to make serious philosophical points. He wanted to free himself from rational thinking by holding ideas up to ridicule.

AL-KINDI

Iraqi philosopher Al-Kindi wanted to find the connection between philosophy and Islam. He was one of the first Islamic scholars to bring ancient Greek ideas to the Islamic world.

c.369–286 BCE

801–873 CE

DAVID HUME

Scottish thinker Hume believed that knowledge was gained through experience. How can we know what a pineapple tastes like if we've never had it before? He also argued against the reliability of science, stating that we can't predict the future based on the past.

1711–1776

JEAN-JACQUES ROUSSEAU

Swiss philosopher Rousseau ran away to France as a teenager. He criticized society because it restricted personal freedoms, and he thought people should be free to choose their own laws. His ideas had a big influence on the French Revolution.

1712–1778

JOHN LOCKE

English philosopher Locke rejected the idea that monarchs had a God-given right to rule, believing instead that power should be given by the people to elected governments. He was forced into exile twice for his revolutionary ideas.

1632–1704

ANNE CONWAY

Although women were banned from studying at universities, English philosopher Anne Conway pursued her philosophy studies regardless, writing letters to her mentor, Cambridge University professor Henry More, on the work of Descartes. Her work was published anonymously after her death.

1631–1679

IBN SINA

Arabic physician Ibn Sina was an expert in medicine and astronomy. He argued that the mind is distinct from the body because a person deprived of all their senses could still think.

c.980–1037

THOMAS AQUINAS

The most famous medieval Christian philosopher, Italian friar Aquinas worked to reconcile the works of ancient Greek thinker Aristotle with the principles of the Christian religion. He was made a saint by the Pope in 1323.

1225–1274

IMMANUEL KANT

This German thinker wanted to understand if human knowledge was limited. He concluded that we'll never know the world as it really is. As we rely on our senses to give us information, we can only ever experience a representation of something, not the thing itself.

1724-1804

JEREMY BENTHAM

Childhood prodigy and English philosopher Bentham founded utilitarianism, a theory that states political decisions should have the aim of achieving the greatest happiness for the greatest number of people.

1748-1832

OLYMPE DE GOUGES

French playwright de Gouges was one of the first feminists. Writing during the French Revolution, she demanded equal rights for women but was left frustrated by the new government's failure to act. She was executed by guillotine for her outspoken views.

1748-1793

RENÉ DESCARTES

French philosopher and scientist Descartes ushered in a new approach to philosophy. He analyzed philosophical questions in the same way a mathematician might tackle a tricky calculation, using logic and evidence.

1596-1650

THOMAS HOBBES

Believing humans to be selfish by nature, English philosopher Hobbes described the need for a "social contract" in which the people give up their personal freedoms in return for protection from an all-powerful monarch.

1588-1679

NICCOLÒ MACHIAVELLI

Italian politician Machiavelli is most famous for his work *The Prince*, in which he offered up practical advice for those in power. For Machiavelli, underhand tactics, such as violence or deceit, were acceptable if these methods helped a ruler achieve their goals.

1469-1527

FRANCIS BACON

English philosopher Francis Bacon believed that scientific knowledge is only possible through observation and experimentation. However, an experiment in food preservation proved his downfall. He died from pneumonia, which he caught while stuffing a chicken with snow.

1561-1626

MARY WOLLSTONECRAFT

A pioneer of early feminism, British writer Wollstonecraft argued that women deserved the same rights as men and equal access to education. She criticized society for not giving women enough opportunities.

1759–1797

JOHN STUART MILL

British thinker Mill thought people should be free to do whatever makes them happy, so long as they don't prevent or harm the happiness of others. He fought for equal rights and championed education for women.

1806–1873

SIMONE DE BEAUVOIR

In her book *The Second Sex*, French writer de Beauvoir criticized society for oppressing women and treating them as separate and inferior to men. She demanded change. At the time, her work demonstrated a radical new way of thinking.

1908–1986

JEAN-PAUL SARTRE

For French thinker Sartre, life was chaotic and meaningless. In his work, he argued that there is no God to give humans a purpose in life, so it is up to us to find our own reasons for existence.

1905–1980

ARNE NAESS

Norwegian philosopher Naess had a big impact on the 20th-century environmental movement. He urged people to stop trying to control nature and instead to "think like a mountain"—to see ourselves as an equal part of the natural world.

1912–2009

PETER SINGER

Champion of animal rights, Australian professor Peter Singer argues that animals should be given "equal consideration" as, just like humans, they are capable of suffering. For Singer, treating animals poorly is a form of discrimination.

1946–

KARL MARX

Along with fellow German philosopher Friedrich Engels, Marx developed communism—a revolutionary theory calling for people to rule themselves and have control of the wealth of their society. The idea inspired the Russian Revolution of 1917.

1818–1883

W.E.B. DU BOIS

Considered by many to be a great social leader, Black American thinker Du Bois was a pragmatist who applied his ideas and writings to the goal of fighting against racial and social inequality.

1868–1963

KARL POPPER

Austrian-born thinker Popper believed that science works by "falsifiability," the idea that no amount of evidence can prove something to be true, as there is always the possibility that a new result will show it to be false.

1902–1994

LUDWIG WITTGENSTEIN

Austrian-born philosopher Wittgenstein was an eccentric who wrote his ideas in notebooks while serving in World War I. He studied the usefulness of language and believed that words only have meaning if a community agrees on how to use them.

1889–1951

BELL HOOKS

Black American professor hooks grew up in a racially divided town in Kentucky. In her writings, she explored how different types of discrimination, such as racism and classism, overlap and reinforce one another, creating multiple layers of injustice.

1952–2021

DJAMILA RIBEIRO

A champion of Black feminism, Black Brazilian philosopher Ribeiro draws attention to the experiences of Black women in Brazil. She highlights social structures that allow Black women to be treated unfairly both for the color of their skin and for their gender.

1980–

GLOSSARY

AFTERLIFE
A life that is lived after death. Different cultures and religions have different beliefs about the afterlife.

ARGUMENT
In philosophy, a set of sentences in which one sentence is being declared to be true (or likely to be true) on the basis of the others.

ARTIFICIAL INTELLIGENCE (AI)
The intelligence demonstrated by a computer system that has been designed to perform tasks that usually require human intelligence.

ASSUMPTION
Something that is thought to be true, even without proof.

BEHAVIOR
The way someone or something acts, especially in response to another person, situation, or event.

BELIEF
An acceptance or trust that something is true, even when it is without evidence.

BIAS
A personal judgment that tends to favor one thing over another, often unfairly.

CLAIM
A statement that something is true.

CONCEPT
A notion or idea.

CONCLUSION
The final part of an argument that is a consequence of the argument's premises.

CONSCIENCE
A person's moral sense of right and wrong. It is said to guide behavior.

CONSCIOUSNESS
An awareness that people have of their own existence and that of the world around them.

CONSEQUENCE
The result of a particular event or action.

CONTEMPORARY
Existing or occurring at the same time; existing or occurring in the present time.

CONTRADICTION
A statement or statements containing ideas that cannot all be true at the same time.

CULTURE
The arts, activities, ideas, customs, and values shared by members of a particular group or society.

DAOISM
An ancient Chinese philosophy. Followers of Daoism believe in living a balanced life that is in harmony with nature.

DEBATE
A discussion between two or more people with different views.

DECEIVE
To deliberately trick someone into believing something that is not true.

DEDUCTION
The method of reasoning from one or more premises to a logically necessary conclusion. See also induction.

DETERMINISM
The view that all events, including human actions, are the result of previous causes; an argument against free will.

DIALOGUE
A conversation between two or more people, sometimes used to look at different sides of a philosophical argument.

DOUBT
In philosophy, the unwillingness to believe something. For example, skeptics doubt that we can ever know anything for sure.

DUTY
A moral or legal task or responsibility.

EMPIRICISM
The view that all knowledge of things that exist outside the mind is acquired through the experiences of the senses.

EQUALITY
When individuals or groups are treated the same way, particularly in regard to legal rights, social status, and pay.

EQUITY
When individuals or groups are given what they need to succeed, rather than everyone being treated the same, particularly in regard to legal rights, social status, and pay.

EXCESS
A large quantity of something that goes beyond what is thought to be proper.

EXISTENCE
The condition of being alive or real.

EXPERIENCE
The knowledge or wisdom someone gains from doing, seeing, or feeling things.

FAIR
When no one is being treated in a way that favors some people over others.

FALLACY
An error in reasoning that results in a false statement.

FALSIFIED
A theory that is proven to be false.

FREE WILL
The power to act by choice without being restricted by outside forces.

FREEDOM
The ability to think, choose, and act for yourself, without restrictions.

HYPOTHESIS
A prediction made on limited evidence that is a starting point for further investigation.

IDEAL
A standard of perfection, beauty, or excellence that something or someone can achieve.

IDENTITY
A person's sense of who they are, often based on characteristics such as gender, appearance, and personality.

ILLUSION
A false belief, or a misinterpreted perception by one or more of the senses.

IMMORTAL
The state of never dying and living forever.

INDUCTION
The method of reasoning that uses past examples to reach a conclusion about the future. *See also* deduction.

INTENTION
A decided course of action, or the determination to act in a certain way.

JUSTIFICATION
An acceptable or good reason for something.

JUSTIFIED
Based on good reasons.

KNOWLEDGE
A belief that must be at least both true and justified.

LIBERTY
The freedoms given to people in a society.

LOGIC
Using reasoning to judge whether something is true or false. Also the branch of philosophy that studies reasoning, including how to construct an argument and identify flaws in arguments.

MORALITY
The standards we use to decide if a belief or action is right or wrong.

NATURE
The basic character of a person or thing.

OBSERVATION
An act of looking at something closely.

OUTCOME
The end result of a behavior, action, or event.

PARTICLE
A tiny component of matter.

PERCEPTION
An awareness of something, such as an object, physical sensation, or event, through the senses.

PHILOSOPHY
A word meaning "love of wisdom," which describes various ways of seeking the truth about ourselves and our lives.

PHYSICAL
Related to things that can be perceived through the senses, as opposed to the mind.

PLEASURE
A happy, satisfied, or delighted feeling.

PREMISE
One of a group of statements in an argument from which a conclusion is made.

PRINCIPLES
A set of rules that explain or control how something works.

PROOF
Evidence, or an argument establishing something to be true.

RATIONAL
Based on clear reasoning.

RATIONALISM
The view that we can gain knowledge of the world through the use of reasoning, without relying on the experiences of our senses.

REASONING
The process of thinking about something in a structured and logical way.

REPRESENT
To portray something in words or images.

RIGHTS
Moral and legal entitlements, such as food, shelter, and equal treatment.

SKEPTICISM
The philosophical position in which the possibility of knowledge is denied or doubted.

SCIENTIFIC METHOD
The way in which scientists discover new facts by testing ideas with experiments.

SELF-CONTROL
The ability to control your impulses, emotions, and actions.

SENSATION
A physical feeling that is picked up by the senses.

SOCIETY
A group of people living together in an organized way according to agreed rules.

SOUL
Also called the mind or spirit. The part of us we think of as "me," which is capable of feeling and thinking. Some philosophers think the soul is separate from the body and will live forever.

STATEMENT
A sentence or claim that can either be true or false.

SUBSTANCE
The material, or matter, that something is made of. In philosophy, also something that can exist without depending on anything else.

THEORY
An idea or a set of rules or principles that is used to explain a fact or event.

THOUGHT EXPERIMENT
An imaginary scenario that allows a philosopher to fully explore a concept or theory.

TRUE
In accordance with fact or reality; genuine, accurate, or exact.

UNIVERSAL
Applies to everyone and everything at all times.

VIRTUAL
Something that exists digitally instead of in the real world.

VIRTUE
An excellent quality in a person, such as courage or honesty.

VOLUNTARY
An action taken by someone of their own free will, rather than by force.

ZOMBIE
In philosophy, a being who seems like a human, but who has no consciousness.

INDEX

ACKNOWLEDGMENTS

DK would like to thank the following people for their assistance in the preparation of this book:

Additional illustrations: Clarisse Hassan; additional text contributions: Zaina Budaly, Marcus Weeks, and Amanda Wyatt; picture research: Niharika Chauhan; Senior Jackets Designer: Suhita Dharamjit; Production Editor: Gillian Reid; proofreading: Victoria Pyke; index: Elizabeth Wise.

The publisher would like to thank the following for their kind permission to reproduce their photographs:

(Key: a-above; b-below/bottom; c-centre; f-far; l-left; r-right; t-top)

10 123RF.com: ssilver (cb). 22 Alamy Stock Photo: Kay Hawkins (br). 33 Getty Images / iStock: Adam Smigielski (tc). 57 Shutterstock.com: FotoRequest (cla). 77 Dreamstime.com: Aaron Amat (cr). 79 Shutterstock.com:

Gorodenkoff (tr). 87 Alamy Stock Photo: DEA / A. VERGANI (cr). 95 Shutterstock.com: Riccardo Mayer (br). 98 Shutterstock.com: TFoxFoto (cr). 105 Alamy Stock Photo: Image Source / Callista Images (br). 113 Dreamstime.com: Toxawww (br). 114 Getty Images / iStock: Stefanie Keller (cra)

All other images © Dorling Kindersley
For further information, see: www.dkimages.com